UNSHAKABLE CERTAINTY

By Dr. James A. Manganiello

ISBN: 0-9760065-0-2

Published by Jones Publishing
Two Center Street
Loft Suite
Groveland, MA 01834

*I DEDICATE THIS BOOK LOVINGLY
TO THE MEMORY OF*

MY MOTHER, CONNIE MANGANIELLO

AND

MY SISTER-IN-LAW, JOAN MANGANIELLO.

THEY ARE SORELY MISSED.

Contents

Preface 7

Acknowledgments 9

Introduction 13

Chapter 1:
First Meeting 31

Chapter 2: Unshakable Certainty Process™, Step 1
Can I Locate Myself? Where Am I? 41

Chapter 3: Unshakable Certainty Process™, Step 2
Can I Breathe Free? 53

Chapter 4: Unshakable Certainty Process™, Step 3
Can I Relocate? 65

Chapter 5: Unshakable Certainty Process™, Steps 4 & 5
Personify and Dialogue 73

Chapter 6:
Connecting The Dots 99

Chapter 7:
Unshakable Certainty & Work 105

Chapter 8:
Unshakable Certainty: Love & Relationship. 121

Chapter 9:
Unshakable Certainty: Health & Well-Being 145

Chapter 10:
Elvis Lives On 169

Appendix 1: Glossary 181

Appendix 2: A Quick and Graphic Summery
of All and Everything 186

Preface

I have spent many years researching the basis of Unshakable Certainty, including a nearly five-year intensive study and secluded practice retreat. Its roots and foundations are something in us that lie beyond fear, doubt and hesitation, something in us that can allow us to live a more creative, more healthy, and a much more fulfilled life.

To discover Unshakable Certainty, you need uncommon knowledge and special tools to put that knowledge to work. I mean for this book to offer you both. I wrote it to give you a reliable map and the means to use that map to find and live a more free, more creative and more self-assured life.

The core of what you'll find within these pages contains the knowledge and a powerful practice that stands free from any inflexible forms, traditions or schools of thought. There is nothing you must believe in, and there's no one you have to follow. The book will show you how to connect to unwavering self-assurance and conviction while you become more of your own guide, mentor and teacher.

I sincerely hope that the book helps and inspires you to see more and be more so you can create the life you want and deserve.

Acknowledgments

I got a good deal of help while writing this book, and I want to acknowledge just some of that help here.

I have the good fortune of having some great friends, guides and teachers whose ideas, support and wisdom allowed me to write a book that turned out a whole lot better than it would have if I relied only on myself.

I want to thank my wife and best friend Wanda for her unwavering love and loyalty and for her good heart, which has become a trusted tuning fork for my own. Through ongoing "meaningful conversations" and collaborations, she helped me to better understand and appreciate what I was writing about.

I owe deep respect and gratitude to H.H. Lungtok Tenpai Nyima—renowned scholar, physician, teacher and head of the remarkable indigenous Tibetan cultural, contemplative and healing tradition known as Yungdrung Bon. His insights, support and encouragement were invaluable to me.

I am indebted to my manager and friend, Errol Smith, a creative pioneer of the first order and founder of Readers Radio Network. His talent, impeccable standards of excellence and his integrity brought the best out of me. Errol's open mind and good heart make his creative genius all the more compelling.

My brother Ed and my nieces Nancy and Maria have opened my eyes wider with their courage, humor and resilience in the face of tragic loss.

I thank my dear friend April Manganiello for her love and

support and for her wise collaboration during some of the early and life changing phases of my research into the seeds of Unshakable Certainty.

My appreciation goes out to Mark Wolper for his steadfast presence and friendship in good times and bad.

The work and writings of Tonpa Shenrab, Hillman, Plotinus, Corbin, Jung and Freud—among others—have especially stirred, challenged and instructed me.

I am grateful to my clients and patients who have been among my greatest teachers. Witnessing their courage and perseverance in pursuing depth and meaning has been a blessing to me.

And finally, I am grateful to Awareness. And to the Wind. I hope to one day repay their kindness.

UNSHAKABLE CERTAINTY

Introduction

"THE PRESENT IS THE ONLY REALITY AND
THE ONLY CERTAINTY."
—SCHOPENHAUER

"IT IS NOT CERTAIN THAT EVERYTHING
IS UNCERTAIN."
—PASCAL

A LITTLE STORY ABOUT JACK, AMY AND GOD

One day God couldn't take Amy and Jack praying to Him any longer. They prayed everyday for so many things that it took God many hours just to listen to them. They wanted to sell their little grocery store in a small town and be able to move into the big city and be free from the constraints of their family, a family that lived in the same small town for five generations.

God came down and met with Jack and Amy. He told them, "I will grant you three wishes and three wishes only. After that, don't bother me anymore. I'm busy." They were thrilled but they were uncertain about exactly what to ask God for. Finally, they decided. For their first wish, they wanted to be so rich that they could leave and start a huge business in New York City while they lived at Trump Towers.

God granted them their wish. However, after a few months they grew homesick. And they were having a lot of complicated business problems; much of their money was at risk. Jack and Amy missed the simple life of their grocery store and the daily connection with their family. They were ready to call God for their second wish, but they were so shaky and uncertain about exactly what to ask for that they were beside themselves.

Amy woke up one morning with a brilliant idea. She told Jack and they called God. "Dearly beloved God", they began, "we are so unsure, confused and frightened about what to ask you for that we've decided that for our second wish we want you to tell us what to ask for—for our third wish."

God laughed out loud. He said, "That's easy. Ask for Unshakable Certainty, then you'll be happy, fulfilled and satisfied no matter what."

LIFE WITH UNSHAKABLE CERTAINTY

How much better would your life be if you were more clear, more steady and more secure about who you are, about your work, about your relationships, and about where your life is going?

Walk with me for a moment and let's consider the difference that Unshakable Certainty could make in your life.

If you had Unshakable Certainty you would live much better than you could possibly live without it. With it, you would be comfortable with yourself in virtually all circumstances. You wouldn't second guess yourself because you would know who you are well enough to understand and accept your own responses to life's challenges.

Your inner trust and self-assurance would allow you to control or eliminate the nagging worries and anxieties that trouble most people. Unshakable Certainty would give you the master key for a deeply satisfying life that could be well-lived, loved and understood.

With Unshakable Certainty, you wouldn't have to battle

with fear, self-doubt, worry, anxiety and depression. As a matter of fact, you would know how to deal with these and other negative states of mind skillfully without becoming identified with or defined by them. Your life could rest on the rock solid self-assurance, security and conviction that only Unshakable Certainty can bring.

With Unshakable Certainty, you could create success in the world from the inside out, success based on your unique and personal vision. You wouldn't burden yourself by dwelling on your failures and shortcomings; instead you would highlight and honor your strengths and successes, and your self-assurance would allow you to build on them. Moreover, your successes wouldn't be just about outside recognition, they would be about inner satisfaction, the kind that bring you the joy of accomplishing things that really mean something and matter to you. Your life and achievements would be pulled from up ahead by your purpose and dreams, instead of being pushed from behind by your fears and worries, or pushed from the side by popular opinion and social pressure.

With Unshakable Certainty you'd be confident that you could deal with whatever comes your way; you would handle people and new situations with ease. You would be able to stand free from guilt, doubt and insecurity, and you would feel good about what you are doing and where you are going. You'd be able to make the high quality choices required to live a high quality life.

Unshakable Certainty would allow you to discover your special gifts and to take the sure and steady action necessary to develop them, action based on an accurate understanding of the forces at play within yourself and of the forces at play outside in the world around you. Self-assurance, deep conviction and integrity would allow you to live life on your own terms while making creative and meaningful decisions rooted in who you deeply are.

Your personal choices would then honor and express your own needs and interests—needs and interests you could guide with a compassionate concern for others and by a desire to make a difference in the world. You'd be able to create a life filled with freedom and with a sense of mission, a life that you'd be very glad to wake up to every day.

UNSHAKABLE CERTAINTY CAN BE YOURS

We are born with a birthright for Unshakable Certainty, but to realize what we're entitled to by birth we have to recognize its value and then find it. If you don't have it today, it's not because you're lacking in some way—you just haven't found it yet. This book will show you <u>exactly</u> how to find and live from it so that you can be more self-assured, comfortable and confident in your own skin and in all areas of your life.

Unshakable Certainty can be yours tomorrow—if you want it. As a clinical psychologist, contemplative practitioner, meditation instructor and consultant to high achievers, I've helped many people find and claim it. In this book, I am going to walk you through a 5-Step Process that will change your life.

As you read you are going to learn how I have helped thousands of people find peace of mind, emotional and mental stability and a sense of Unshakable Certainty about who they are and how they can make the very most of their lives. I've spent 30 years developing, testing and perfecting this very powerful, life-enhancing practice.

This 5-Step Process is easy to learn and use; you can use it anywhere, anytime. It will give you what you need to connect to who you deeply are so you can find the conviction and confidence you need to live more clearly and more powerfully. Before we turn toward the Process, let's look for a moment at what life is like without Unshakable Certainty.

LIFE WITHOUT UNSHAKABLE CERTAINTY

If you are shaky and uncertain in your life, one thing is for sure—it won't be satisfying or a lot of fun. Here's why. Your life will be made small by fear, self-doubt and hesitation. Without Unshakable Certainty, you'll live in recurring doubt about who you are, about your work and relationships, and about what your life means and should be all about. Your life will feel a bit like something you just don't have the manual or the tools to make work properly.

You'll experience conflict and confusion on a regular basis. In the morning you might feel OK about your marriage or your work and your approach to life only to have the sands shift by noon when you feel just as sure that your marriage is wrong or that you should have left your well-paying, but uninteresting job to do other more meaningful work. Then the next hour or day, you can feel completely different again; your values will tend to shift so much that you won't be sure what to believe any longer. You can find yourself at the mercy of your last state of mind or of the last expert you listened to or book you read.

And as if all this wasn't bad enough, without Unshakable Certainty, you'll feel more stressed out, bored and bummed out, and as a result you'll be more vulnerable to health problems that limit and that can even shorten your life. Shaky uncertainty generates a lot of chronic stress and unhappiness, an awful combination and one that causes illness and that claims many lives each year.

Here's just a sample of what shaky uncertainty can look like, stated in the simple form of conflicting positions. In reality, our inner conflicts can take more complicated forms and involve three, four or more opposing positions.

* I need to stop working so much and enjoy the things that really make life worth living.
* I need to focus more on my work or I will lose my benefits and have financial trouble.

* My life is an adventure; I need to take risks.
* My life is really a dangerous train ride; I need to be very careful.

* I can go out on my own and make more money doing what I really want to do.
* I am fooling myself; I have limits—I need to stay put and be grateful I have a good job.

* I should save, save, save for retirement.
* I should spend, do and have more now and enjoy life while I can.

* I should set more fixed limits with my kids and help better guide them.
* I should allow my kids to be free to make their own mistakes and find their own way.

* I know how to be a good parent; I am doing a nice job.
* I don't know how to parent my children; I need to get help before I damage them.

* Of course God exists; I should be more religious.
* There's no God; I'm foolish to believe that there is.

* My sexual desires are just free and wild.
* My sexual desires prove that there's something wrong with me.

And so on, and on and on.

If you lack Unshakable Certainty, you'll tend to avoid the risks of learning how to do what's necessary to live a more exciting, more creative and more rewarding life—but it won't be because you don't want to. You'll want a better life, but because you'll doubt that your efforts to have one will be successful, you won't act to create what you want. You may want badly to cross the street, but if you don't believe and expect that your legs will get you there—you're not going to take that first step. With shaky uncertainty clarity is not possible, and doubt and hesitation will leave you standing still while your life just drives by.

If you are shaky and uncertain, recurring moods of self-doubt, confusion and inner conflict, and the worry, indecision and resentment that come with these moods, will force you to play it safe. Like a big corporation that has its worried eyes glued on the short-term bottom line, we miss the big rewards that life can deliver if we live it as a long-term adventure—rather than as an occasion to avoid short-term risk.

Your biggest danger is that shaky uncertainty will keep you trapped in an identity and in a life that's too small for who you truly are. Then you'll become more like a passenger than a driver on the road of your life. You'll do what you feel you should and must, not what you really want and love, and worse still, without deep self-assurance and conviction—you might never even discover what you truly want and love

A SMALL SAMPLE OF LIVES LIVED IN UNCERTAINTY

What follows is a small sample of stories about some of the people I've worked with over the years. They show a brief glimpse of what we're talking about, about the discomfort, confusion and limitations that come with the territory of shaky uncertainty. Let's take a quick look at them for perspective.

Getting fired sent Carolyn Nevis into a depression that put her to bed for an entire month...whenever Greg Saunder's boss called him into his office, Greg felt like a quivering mass...Tom Johnson's confrontations with his wife Michelle made him feel like an indentured servant with no legitimate voice of his own...Raymond Lilly felt hopeless and helpless much of the time and often wondered whether life was worth living...

Diane Falco spent many years getting educated and trained as a neurologist but she hates her work; she is afraid to make any changes, and she drinks too much...Bill and Cindy Murphy got so wealthy their great, great grandchildren won't have to work, but they are mostly bored and anxious much of the time, and they quarrel a lot...Rich Greenburg is a very lonely attorney who has been divorced four times; he feels like a complete failure....

And finally, the Coopers are like many people. They're a married couple doing well; nothing is noticeably wrong, they make good money and have children and friends—but deep down they feel as if someone else wrote the screenplay for their lives, lives that just don't feel right....

These are small scenes from lives lived without the self-assurance, clarity and conviction. You can avoid this level of life, if you really want to. You can claim the flexibility and resilience that comes with living life with firm conviction and self-assurance—if you know how to find Unshakable Certainty

Before we explore exactly how to do it, let's look first at how not to do it.

THE MIRAGE OF EXTERNAL SUCCESS

One inauthentic style of dealing with shaky uncertainty is to try to negate it through achievement. Those who do this flee from a lot of self-doubt and insecurity, but just barely. They stay just a step ahead of it, like someone fleeing from an angry dog that's right behind them. The angry dog of shaky uncertainty can chase many people into a fierce struggle for power, position and wealth. It's important that you avoid this seductive struggle because it's a false path; it doesn't deliver what it promises.

As a consultant to many hundreds of high achievers, I've worked with a lot of people who fall into this category. They reason that great financial success and recognition will conquer their doubt and uncertainty. They place huge bets that achieving wealth and power will free them from uncertainty and that the payoff will be a life of relaxed ease and satisfaction.

Many folks work hard to achieve great success and huge wealth because they are driven to do so. But very often it's a half-hearted, external success only, not an inside-out success, not a success flowing from a deeply felt certainty about who they are and what their lives are uniquely about. Unlike the successes of someone who has found Unshakable Certainty, theirs are driven from behind by the attacking dog of their insecurities, not pulled up ahead by their dreams and visions for tomorrow.

Our culture tends to reward this kind of effort to medicate fear and self-doubt by seeking certainty outside of oneself. It doesn't matter how you get to rich and powerful, as long as you get to rich and powerful. But as Lily Tomlin told us—even if we win the rat race—we're still a rat. Big time outside success always markets and promotes itself as a great antidote for our self-doubt and insecurity—but it never turns out to be that. It's not a good remedy for shaky uncertainty at all.

It may be better to be rich, powerful and poisoned than to be just poisoned, but surely not that much better. And people who lack Unshakable Certainty who achieve external success have the added burden of having to face that they have been misled, that they have spent long and often tortuous hours marching in the heat of many a noonday sun—toward a mirage.

After they get their sought after success, they often discover that there's no deep relief or satisfaction in it. They're still under attack by the same old feelings, but now with a different agenda of concerns. "Was I just lucky? Will I be found out? Can I do it again? Will I lose my position, my wealth...and so on and on and on."

The uncertainty monsters don't go away if we get rich and powerful; they just drive in more expensive cars and live in more expensive homes. Before we move on to discover the real basis for deep self-assurance, conviction, joy and happiness, let's take a look at another kind of certainty mirage. The human mind seems especially vulnerable to being seduced by this one. Let's keep our eyes open to recognize how widespread this mirage is today, and perhaps we can even see the parts of ourselves that may be drawn to it.

SIMPLE SOLUTIONS AND THE PEOPLE WHO SELL THEM: THE MIRAGE OF DOGMATIC POSITIONS AND IDEALIZED LEADERS

The rat race for wealth and success is not the only way people try to medicate the pain of pervasive fear, doubt and insecurity. There are other dead ends. The fact is that most people who seek unwavering certainty and deep conviction without benefit of a good map and the right knowledge and tools often lose their way trying to find it.

Looking for certainty in dogmatic fixed beliefs and the idealized leaders who promote them is a good illustration of just how lost we can get. Shaky uncertainty can be so uncomfortable for us that it moves us to grab hold of narrow, fixed beliefs that appear firm and definite just so we can feel a sense of order and control in our lives. In the extreme, we can become passionately attached to these fixed positions as a guiding light, a light that we fantasize will lead us to relief from chaos, worry and self-doubt.

Becoming "true believers", many people pledge loyalty and commitment to dogmatic ideas for the chance to feel they are a part of something true, great and right, for the chance to be or know something that allows them to feel superior to others and so more certain in their lives.

Political and religious dogmas are magnets for all true believers, including the true believers that may live in us. Supporters and advocates of the political left or the right can be seen regularly on TV making self-righteous pronouncements and holier than thou statements with expressions of scorn and intolerance all over their faces.

History teaches us a harsh lesson: Among frightened and insecure people, dogmatic beliefs can spread like a viral infection, unconsciously infecting them with false and even delusional ideas that they experience as true and sane. If we get infected by such a virus, we can become devoted to a charismatic figure and to his or her dogmatic all-knowing ideas. The cult of personality around figures such as Mao, Stalin, Hitler and Napoleon, as well as many lesser figures alive and in our midst today, illustrate how easy it is for people—many of them just like you or me—to become true believers and blindly follow idealized personalities in search of absolute conviction and certainty.

Charismatic figures can attract us if we're looking for an all-powerful guide and role model to lead us out of the terribly uncomfortable desert of uncertainty. The fact is that anyone troubled by self-doubt, fear and insecurity can become strongly drawn to the experience of certainty that comes with following a leader; followers feel better and they get energized by the borrowed dreams and the borrowed sense of purpose they get from an appealing and captivating leader. Little do they realize that the larger than life charismatic leader is almost always concerned about himself, not about them or even about the causes or ideas they champion and promote. The fact is that unless a powerful leader has achieved authentic Unshakable Certainty, he or she will seek power over others as a means of keeping his or her own uncertainty monsters at bay.

Powerful leaders are usually after their own glory, power and certainty first and foremost. As Napoleon noted, "If I lose my throne I will bury the world beneath my ruins." And Hitler's wicked madness shone through clearly in his statement: "I have to gain immortality, even if the whole German nation perishes."

Lesser examples abound in everyday life. We need to be wide awake to our own tendencies to embrace narrow and inflexible positions, and the leaders that market them, to ease our fear and insecurity, especially in times of trouble and danger.

Like running after wealth and power, seeking Unshakable Certainty in dogmatic beliefs or in idealized leaders is a mirage—in the long term these ideas and leaders can never deliver what they promise.

A FINAL NOTE ON MIRAGES

We could imagine Unshakable Certainty as a destination that we want to get to. We might think that achievement and great wealth will get us there or that embracing dogmatic ideas and leaders will get us there. But they won't.

It's not that there's anything inherently wrong with achievement and ambition, or with having strong passionate beliefs about important ideas or with admiring the people who speak and stand for these ideas. The point is that these things become mirages or wrong roads only when we use them as a means to find Unshakable Certainty.

In truth, Unshakable Certainty can energize dedicated work and high levels of achievement and it can inspire our embrace of noble ideas and ideals. People with unwavering conviction don't just sit around detached from life. They are doers; they create and act powerfully from their convictions, on behalf of others, and they make a difference in the world.

We need a reliable map to get to Unshakable Certainty; it can only be found in a place that is genuinely beyond fear, doubt and hesitation. This book is about learning and doing what's necessary to find the firm and steady self-assurance, freedom and conviction that will genuinely change your life.

IMAGINE YOUR LIFE WITH UNSHAKABLE CERTAINTY

Take a few moments and imagine how your life would look, feel and be like if you had Unshakable Certainty. Can you feel the smile it will put on your inner face? It's a smile of deep fulfillment and happiness, a smile that reflects your inner security and peace of mind, one that mirrors your joy at living from unwavering conviction and confidence. It's an inner smile that only comes with knowing and accepting who you truly are.

The difference between your life lived in doubt and hesitation and your life lived in Unshakable Certainty is the difference between night and day. Your life with Unshakable Certainty is lived as an adventure of love, courage and wisdom. Unshakable Certainty is an inner wealth that enables you to deal with whatever comes your way. It arises from a state of mind that's like a lion's roar in the deep jungle, a roar that signals that all situations are workable.

HOW YOU CAN FIND UNSHAKABLE CERTAINTY

So how can you find Unshakable Certainty? What do you need to know and do to live with the steady self-assurance and deep conviction?

This book will give you the uncommon knowledge you need to answer these questions, along with the powerful tools to learn exactly what you must do to find and live from Unshakable Certainty. Let me introduce you to the territory we'll be working in. Our first task is to understand the true sources of the fear, self-doubt and hesitation that hold us back and that keep us from enjoying a better quality life. Where does our insecurity and uncertainty really come from? Just why do we often feel confused and in doubt about who we are, about what we do and about the choices we make? Finding answers to these questions is necessary and inspiring.

We also need to discover the real basis of genuine Unshakable Certainty. What is it rooted in? What's its foundation and support, and what do we need to do to find it and then to strengthen our connection to it and finally in due course, to make it a part of our lives?

UNCOMMON KNOWLEDGE AND THE UNSHAKABLE CERTAINTY PROCESS™

To answer these questions and find the real basis for self-assurance and deep conviction, we're going to learn and use a powerful practice, The Unshakable Certainty Process™.

I created, tested and perfected the Process during 30 years of research and intense work—work with patients in my clinical practice, work in the psychological and contemplative sciences and work in the inner growth and well-being traditions. The Process can allow you and empower you to find Unshakable Certainty. Each time you practice the UC Process™ properly, you'll free yourself from shaky and uncertain states of mind. As you become skilled and proficient in using it, you can access the state of mind that is utterly beyond doubt and insecurity.

With repeated experiences of this deep connection to who you most deeply are, to Unshakable Certainty, your characteristic mood or View will become more calm, clear and self-assured and your life will change accordingly.

The book explains and illustrates this 5-Step practice in detail so you'll be able to grasp and appreciate its power as quickly as possible.

SUMMING UP

Unshakable Certainty will allow you to be more clear, more steady and more secure about who you are, about your work, about your relationships and about where your life is going. It will greatly improve the quality of your life, making you more satisfied and fulfilled while at the same time protecting your health and well-being.

The Unshakable Certainty Process™ is a powerful practice that will lead you directly to the true basis for unshakable self-assurance, conviction, security, joy, peace and serenity.

Let's now turn to what we need to know to make our way....

CHAPTER 1
First Meeting

"WE ARE DISTURBED NOT BY THINGS, BUT BY THE VIEW WHICH
WE TAKE OF THEM."
—EPICTETUS

"KNOWLEDGE...IS THE BEGINNING OF HAPPINESS."
—SANTAYANA

Let's now meet the ideas we'll be working with throughout the book. They provide the facts, information and knowledge you'll need to make your way to Unshakable Certainty, and they will shed light on the Process, so you can see clearly what it is and why using it skillfully is so important, powerful and necessary.

Our goal in this chapter is to make you familiar with these important ideas and with their relationship to one another and to Unshakable Certainty. Then in the coming chapters, you will be better able to appreciate their significance, especially while you learn to use the Process. Here are the ideas:

- Location, View and Reality
- Waking Dreams
- Self-Image
- Surface Identity
- Wrong Psychological Address
- Briar Patches
- Mapping
- Safeguard
- Steadfast Knowledge
- True Psychological Address
- Innermost Identity

- The Free Position
- Aware Presence

Location, View and Reality (LVR) Location is perhaps the most important idea in the book that you must really get. To borrow a notion from the real estate professionals, there are three things you need to understand to be able to find and live from Unshakable Certainty: Location, Location and Location.

If you understand Location, everything else will fall into place quite nicely. Location is where we are in any given moment; it's the answer to the question: What state of mind am I in right now? Or put more simply: Where am I now? View is what we see from where we are, and Reality is our experience that gets defined by what we see.

If you understand LVR, you'll understand three very important things:

- Your Location determines your View.
- Your View defines your Reality.
- Your Reality is your experience of what is real.

The Unshakable Certainty Process™ (the UC Process™ or the Process) is so powerful because it makes us aware of our Location, View and Reality, moment to moment, so we can stay awake while kayaking in the river of our life. If you're not awake, you won't know where you are going or when or how to paddle to arrive at a worthwhile destination. Sudden shifts in your Location, in your state of mind, can throw you off course, into confusion and even into danger. Sudden shifts can toss you into **Waking Dreams**, dreams in which the monsters of self-doubt, hesitation and uncertainty attack you at your most vulnerable spots.

We have Waking Dreams all the time. They happen whenever we're not aware of where we are (our Location). During sleep when you dream that a fierce monster is chasing you, you flee in dread and horror. Why? Because your dream View is that you're in danger. You're dreaming, but you're not aware of it. Once you wake up, your Location shifts to "awake" and your View and Reality shift accordingly. No need to look for the monsters under the bed. You <u>know</u> they don't really exist.

Similarly, you can fall into Waking Dreams during the day, dreams in which your fear, self-doubt and insecurity "monsters" chase you around—when you don't realize "where you are". That is, when you don't realize that <u>your Location is a state of mind,</u> one among others, with a fear and self-doubt View. When you're unaware that you're in a Waking Dream, you mistake these dream monsters as <u>real</u> ones. That View then defines your Reality and what you experience is shaky uncertainty. The Unshakable Certainty Process™ will help you to avoid and awaken from your Waking Dreams; it will help you to live at another level, a level where you don't have to spend so much time fleeing from monsters that are not really there.

Self-Image We develop our self-image in our family. We come to see ourselves as we were seen by others during critical periods in our formative years. Your self-image is a surface affair, conditioned by your family and your culture. It's made up from borrowed and downloaded ideas about who you are, about your physical and psychological characteristics, about your intelligence and abilities and about your value and worthiness as a human being. Although your Self-Image is largely formed and conditioned by others' Views of you, you still come to think of it as who you really are, as your "I" or "me". It becomes your **Wrong Psychological Address**, a place where you reside much of the time, but one which isn't your true home. It's not where you belong, but you don't realize that—yet.

The truth is that our Self-Image is so powerful that whether or not it's accurate —we think, feel and act in accord with it. This fact has caused at least as much suffering and as much wasted life as war. Self-Image is like a mask we put on but can't get off. To make matters worse, we typically forget that we put it on. It can cause a lot of pain, wasted life and Waking Dreams that leave us adrift in a sea of emotional confusion and wrong assumptions about who we are and about what our life can be.

A client of mine made a comment that has stayed with me for many years. After finally waking up from her Surface Identity, from her Wrong Address, she said:

> "I feel as if I put a mask on 30 years ago and then I
> forgot all about it—and then I forgot that I forgot—
> until I really found myself again."

That mask that we all put on is our conditioned Self-Image, and as long as we are located there, we're stuck living in cramped quarters. You must become aware of your conditioned Self-Image as the Location of your **Surface Identity**, because if you are to find Unshakable Certainty, you need to move beyond it because it's not who you really are. You need to become aware of its habitual Views by discovering, studying and understanding them so you can free yourself from its conditioned limits. You can <u>never</u> find Unshakable Certainty while stuck at your Wrong Address.

Our Surface Identity carries with it fear, doubt and hesitation because <u>they are its nature.</u> Shaky uncertainty comes with its territory. You are not afraid and hesitant and unsure of yourself because you are lacking in some way. It's not <u>you</u> that's the problem, though you may feel convinced that you are.

Thinking that insecurity and uncertainty are your fault is a costly misunderstanding, one that reflects a lack of awareness of the nature and power of Location, View and Reality. When you are in Seattle in the winter, you get wet; it comes with the territory, with the Location. When you are located at your Wrong Address, at your Surface Location, then fear, doubt, and hesitation are your View and your experience of Reality. They too come with the territory.

Here's a glimpse of our dilemma. Our conditioned Surface Identity, our "I" or "me" is all we know, and because it <u>appears</u> to be who we are, we wrongly conclude that it must be. But the earth appears flat and it's not, and the sun appears to rise, but it doesn't—so we need to really be open the possibility that <u>we are more than we appear to be to ourselves.</u>

Our **Briar Patches** are the patches of unseen and unknown emotional territory within our own mind that we can fall into and get stuck in. We get stuck in them so easily because they're filled with the thorny hurts, wounds and feelings from past time, with unfinished business that lies outside of our awareness.

A Briar Patch lies dormant within our mind until it's triggered by an inner or outer event. Then it comes to life and we fall into it in an instant, without realizing what's happening. A Briar Patch is a Location and because we're usually unaware that we've fallen into it, we become identified with or swallowed up by its View and Reality.

When we fall into and get stuck in Briar Patch Locations, we don't know it; the fall happens so suddenly, and we're quickly thrown into powerful feelings that seem to be here and now, but they're not. If our parents disciplined us with guilt when we were young, for example, and if our spouse or friend lays a little guilt on us today, we'll go ballistic because our anger from there and then will leak into here and now—<u>without our real-</u>

izing it. And so our present will carry the weight from our past.

This is a form of Waking Dream; we're simply not aware of where we are within ourselves. **Mapping** our Briar Patch Locations is essential. If we don't Map these Locations, then when we fall into them we'll get swept up in their Views and the experiences of Reality they define. Then we'll be vulnerable to Briar Patch based Waking Dreams, dreams that leave us feeling shaky and uncertain.

When we Map a Briar Patch, we learn where it is, what it looks like and how it operates in our thought and feeling. If you owned 10 acres of land and you mapped it, you'd observe and chart its territory so you'd know where it is, what's on it and what the view is from there. Similarly, when you Map your Briar Patches, you observe and study them to become aware of what's "in them" and when and how what's in them affects you. In this way, you develop self-knowledge and awareness of your Briar Patches as Locations, each with their own particular View and experience of Reality.

The Unshakable Certainty Process™ is a powerful tool for Mapping Briar Patches and all conditioned states of mind, including your Self-Image. When you use the Process to Map your Briar Patches you'll come face to face with **Safeguard**. Safeguard represents the security and protection forces within your personality.

Safeguard is like a dear friend who acted on our behalf when as children we were in psychological trouble. He turned the volume down on any emotional experiences that threatened your ability to hold it together, such as fear for example. By cutting you off from overwhelming amounts of fear, Safeguard could protect you from hurt, harm, and from becoming undone.

But your fear didn't go away. It just got stored in your unconscious mind—it's now a Briar Patch—one from past time that you can fall into whenever you feel fear in present time circumstances. Briar Patches can leave you feeling unsteady and uncertain at any moment.

The problem with Safeguard is that he is stuck in past time and so he keeps us stuck there as well. He's like a soldier who doesn't know that the war is over. He'll keep you fighting battles in a war that ended long ago unless he learns what he needs to know to come into present time.

It's up to **Steadfast Knowledge** to bring Safeguard into present time. As you use the Unshakable Certainty Process™ you become more aware, and you begin to awaken to what's actually going on. As you awaken, you gather knowledge, experiential self-knowledge. This self-knowledge gradually comes to life as a stable center of gravity within you; it comes to life as Steadfast Knowledge. Remember this: Steadfast Knowledge is the Mother of Unshakable Certainty.

Once Steadfast Knowledge educates Safeguard, she liberates him from the prison of past time Locations and obsolete Views. Safeguard then loosens his grip and gives us easier access to our Briar Patches so we can Map and heal them properly. As we do, we learn how to stand free from the negative states of mind that breed insecurity and self-doubt.

Steadfast Knowledge ultimately teaches you that your Self-Image is not who you really are, and she helps you to discover and recognize the Location of your **Innermost Identity.** Your Innermost Identity is who you truly are, in your deepest being; it's where you find genuine self-confidence based on the ability to simply be who you are.

Like the sun that's blocked from View on a cloudy day, who we deeply are is not visible to us when our Surface Identity is in the way. Once you develop the eyes to see through and beyond your Surface Identity, you'll discover a deeper essence within

yourself that is your **True Psychological Address.** Your True
Address, your Innermost Identity gives you access to the **Free
Position** and to **Aware Presence**, two sides of the same coin.

The Free Position is the Unshakable Certainty Location; it
is wide open and without fixed Views of any kind. Its Reality is
always—clear, calm, and aware. When you are in the Free
Position, you are aware and present—you're awake—here and
now.

The common View is that confidence and certainty come
from inner toughness; from unwavering will and determina-
tion. This is an illusion and these things can just be muscle flex-
ing from our Wrong Address, a Location that remains our
Wrong Address, no matter how well we clean, furnish and for-
tify it.

Surface Identity certainty is always at risk and temporary,
because it's a short lived affair dependent upon definite conditions being in place. Innermost Identity certainty, in contrast, is
independent of any conditions; it's always completely secure
and unshakable. Why? Because it's a state of mind that lies
beyond fear, self-doubt and uncertainty. It's based on the awareness that comes with being connected to who we actually are.

Think of it this way. Ordinary certainty is like having a
good dream. Everything is working well and going fine and so
we feel self-assured, confident and secure. But if the dream turns
bad, if it turns toward trouble, then uncertainty creeps back in.

In contrast, Unshakable Certainty remains unshakable no
matter which way things turn, because we are aware that it's a
dream. When you're able to be aware in the dream, its story
line cannot possess you by defining your View and experience
of Reality. You are aware and awake—and so you are free. This
capacity to be awake in your dreams— allows your certainty to
remain steadfast no matter what happens.

Something very similar happens in our waking life. Once we have connected to our Innermost Location, we find the Free Position and Aware Presence. Unshakable Certainty is this aware sense of presence; it allows us to remain aware and awake in any and all of our Waking Dreams.

When you find Unshakable Certainty, it's not that you won't ever encounter fear, self-doubt and hesitation. It's that you'll remain awake in the face of these feelings, like being awake in a nighttime dream. If you are connected to your True Address, to the Aware Presence that comes with it, then you can remain awake in the face of all kinds of uncertainty weather: fear and self-doubt, insecurity, hesitation and so on.

If you are awake in relationship to these feelings, then you won't mistake them for facts. If you don't mistake these feelings for facts, then they won't "possess" you by defining your Reality. The capacity to be awake is what enables certainty to remain steadfast no matter what happens.

<u>This is the key to Unshakable Certainty.</u>

Now we're ready to turn to the Unshakable Certainty Process™. It will show us exactly what we need to know and do to find this extraordinary possibility in our lives.

CHAPTER 2

The Unshakable Certainty Process™

STEP 1

Can I Locate Myself?
Where Am I?

"WHAT IS NECESSARY TO CHANGE A PERSON IS TO CHANGE HIS AWARENESS OF HIMSELF."

—MASLOW

"LET US NOT LOOK BACK IN ANGER OR FORWARD IN FEAR, BUT AROUND IN AWARENESS."

—JAMES THURBER

"TO BECOME DIFFERENT FROM WHAT WE ARE, WE MUST HAVE SOME AWARENESS OF WHAT WE ARE."

—ERIC HOFFER

"EVEN A LITTLE EFFORT TOWARD ... AWARENESS WILL PROTECT YOU FROM THE GREATEST FEAR.

—BHAGAVAD GITA

THE UNSHAKABLE CERTAINTY PROCESS™

Step 1	Step 2	Step 3	Step 4	Step 5
CAN I LOCATE MYSELF? WHERE AM I?	Can I Breathe Free?	Can I Relocate?	Personify	Dialogue

PERSPECTIVE ON LEARNING THE PROCESS

This book will give you a clear explanation of each of the five Steps in the Unshakable Certainty Process™, and you can feel free to experiment with them on your own—as long as you feel comfortable while doing so. The book's instructions are clear and comprehensive enough for you to experience the power of what the Process can bring to your life.

If you want to experience the greatest benefits that the Process can offer you however, then you need expert instruction, training and guidance (something we'll explore later in the book).

The Unshakable Certainty Process™ is a clear and reliable path to unwavering self-assurance, confidence and conviction. Learning the Process is like learning a dance. Once you get each of the steps of a particular dance down, then you can do that dance—without thinking too much about it.

It's easier and more reliable to learn a dance expertly when someone who knows how to do that dance shows you the steps and trains you how to do them properly. Then you can be certain that you have each step down correctly. And you can go off on your own and perfect what you have learned with the utmost confidence in what you are doing. With the right instruction and dedicated practice, the Process will become easy and natural. It will become like a graceful dance that you can do without having to think about how to do it.

Once you get the Steps down, then you can use the Process in your everyday life. It's not something that you have to do only at set times or in special places; that's part of the beauty and power of the practice. You can use it anytime, anywhere—while you are on the phone, in a meeting, in face to face conversation, in traffic and so on. You can use it whenever you're feeling fear, self-doubt, insecurity or hesitation. You can use it when you feel the grip of a depressed or a stressed out state of mind that leaves you shaky and uncertain.

The Process will lead you to Unshakable Certainty, and it will serve as your Broadband connection to the self-assurance, conviction, confidence and inner trust that comes from being deeply connected to who you truly are.

Practicing the Process will sustain this connection and it will:

- keep you from being defined by fear, doubt and hesitation;
- take much of the guess work out of your life;
- allow you to feel more sure about who you are and about what you're doing with your life and why;
- give you a confidence that you can handle pretty much any situation that comes your way;
- vastly improve your work and relationship life;
- protect your health and well-being; and
- give you more joy, peace and happiness doing the things that really make life worth living.

Just remember that sometimes everyone feels awkward when learning a "new dance." If you have any performance Briar Patches (sensitive past wounds around performance issues that most of us have), they'll probably come up when you begin to learn the Process. So be alert and offer yourself friendship, generosity and support; then you'll be able to learn it well and get a taste of the tremendous benefits that Unshakable Certainty will bring to your life. Don't strain—practice with a light touch and joyful effort.

The Process has 5 Steps, as follows:

- Can I <u>L</u>ocate Myself? Where Am I?
- Can I <u>B</u>reathe Free?
- Can I <u>R</u>elocate?
- Personify
- Dialogue

Let's move now to meet and learn Step 1: Can I Locate Myself? Where Am I?

STEP 1

Step 1 is like a wake up call that we give to ourselves. The questions: Can I Locate myself now? Where am I?—are calls or signals that you can use to become aware of your Location, View and Reality (LVR). Recall that if you don't know what LVR you're in, then you're in a Waking Dream.

Imagine that you are asleep in your bed dreaming. You're dreaming that you're driving to work in your car. While you are dreaming, the dream is your Location, driving to work is your View, and your Reality is the experience that comes with the territory of driving to work. You feel in a "driving to work mood"; you notice the familiar scenery and so on.

Now imagine that I come to your bedroom door and I call your name. I call your name once and then a second time. My voice calling your name the second time wakes you up. When you awaken, you are no longer dreaming. Your Location changed from the dream "I am driving to work" to "I was asleep dreaming, Jim called my name and now I am lying in my bed at home."

When you use Step 1 you are like Jim who comes to your

door and calls your name. Whatever state of mind you were in before you did Step 1 (before you come to your door and call your own name) felt literally and factually real to you. But once you're aware and awake, you realize that your state of mind, including fear, self-doubt and insecurity, is just a state of mind and not a factual reality.

Our feelings are not facts; they don't necessarily testify to literal truth. In time, you'll see again and again that all states of mind are Locations with particular Views and experiences of Reality.

Let's remind ourselves of something before we go on. We noted in Chapter 1 that there were three critically important things we need to know about Location. Let's revisit this knowledge here so we can keep them in mind.

The three things you need to know about Location are:

- Your Location determines your View.
- Your View defines your Reality.
- Your Reality is your experience of what is real.

We can now see Step 1 of the Unshakable Certainty Process™ more clearly—as a tool we use to put this knowledge to work. Step 1 helps you to stay alert and awake. You practice by asking yourself the questions: Can I Locate Myself Now? Where Am I? With practice these questions will bring an immediate experience of awareness. This awareness is an opportunity to recognize that any state of mind you are in is not literal or factual truth; it's a Location with a View and an Experience of Reality that is relative to that Location.

This awareness can make a powerful difference in your life because it cuts through uncertainty before it takes deep root. It prevents fear, self-doubt and insecurity from establishing themselves as "the truth." Let's use an illustration to demonstrate just how powerful Step 1 can be.

Imagine that I am interviewing in a few days for an important new job as a psychologist.

On the morning of the interview I'm flooded by shaky uncertainty, I feel afraid that I am not really good enough for the job and I doubt my abilities. I feel that I am not qualified and I hesitate to even try to toot my own horn, because I feel insecure about myself and about how others will see me. It gets so bad that I actually lose touch with my strengths and why I truly deserve the job, and with the fact that I am a very capable psychologist.

Now without an understanding of LVR and without Step 1, this flood of uncertainty will feel very real to me, as if it testified to truths about who I am, and I would mistake these feelings for facts. I might even decide to back out of the interview. Or at best, I would show up as a much smaller version of who I really am, and so chances are I wouldn't get the job.

To make matters even worse, I'd conclude that I didn't get the job because I wasn't good enough. This is a brutal but fairly common Waking Dream. It's actually a daytime version of a nightmare. But I wouldn't ever realize that it was a Waking Dream—unless I became aware and woke up from it.

Step 1 of the Process does just that: It will awaken you from the hell of starring in Waking Dreams filled with shaky uncertainty monsters. Let's see how.

Step 1 is like someone at my door calling my name waking me up from a dream. Once awake, I release from the dream story line. It no longer defines my reality. I can stand free of it.

When the flood of uncertainty comes in the form of fear and self-doubt about my credentials and worthiness, it now signals me to ask: "Can I Locate Myself? Where Am I Now?" A sliver of awareness suddenly registers that I am in a Location with fear and self-doubt as the View, and with uncertainty as the Reality.

This sliver of awareness immediately wakes me up and frees me from the misconception that my fear and self-doubt testify to truth or fact—they are just a LVR. That sliver of awareness that becomes conscious of what is going on is separate from what's going on—it becomes my new Location.

The View and Reality from the awareness Location is open and free; it has no agenda. It's just awareness. It's not invested in or attached to whether or not I get the job. That's how free it is. From this Location I too am free—free to be who I am. It's beyond the hope that I will get the job and the fear that I won't. This awareness is the core of Unshakable Certainty. If I get the job—fine. If I don't—that's fine too. It's not that I don't care, it's that I am aware enough not to slip into desperation or neurotic worry. I'll do my best to check things out and to present myself, but my well-being does not depend on my getting the job. It depends on my being aware.

While in the beginning, it may take experience and additional Steps of the Process to awaken you to this level, at the very least, Step 1 makes you aware of what's going on. It allows you to instantly know that when you are flooded by self-doubt and worry, you're in a Location with a self-doubt and worry View. If you can be aware, then the feelings of uncertainty will lose power over you. Because there is a world of difference between being in a dream in which a monster is chasing you (fear, self-doubt) and being in a dream that <u>you know is a dream</u>. The instant you become aware that you are dreaming, you will feel assurance that you are not in danger, because awareness is now your new Location. Let's take a closer look at this key point.

ONCE YOU KNOW YOUR LOCATION, AWARENESS BECOMES YOUR NEW LOCATION

When you suddenly remember to do Step 1, a part of you wakes up from being identified with or possessed by a Location. It's as if a part of you steps off the stage of whatever state of mind you're in. That part of you is a sliver of awareness and it moves into the audience front row center; it moves into a position where it can see what's going on. Your awareness sees your "on stage Location" from an entirely free and separate point of View.

This sliver of awareness just sees and knows; it doesn't judge, praise or blame. I am now Located in awareness itself. As Francis of Assisi put it so very well, "What you are looking for is what is looking."

Losing this awareness by becoming identified with the fixed point of View in any Location is the foundation for uncertainty. When you're aware that you are dreaming and you know that the story line is not literally real, then you are free from the dream story line as a fixed point of View. Being aware and standing free from any fixed point is the foundation of Unshakable Certainty. With Unshakable Certainty, you can "host" any state of mind you are in as if it were a visitor.

As we practice Step 1, we begin to shift from uncertainty based states of mind that we take literally like we do when we're in a dream and don't know it, to increasing degrees of certainty-based awareness, like we do when we recognize we're dreaming and we wake up.

MAPPING AND GROWING
STEADFAST KNOWLEDGE

As you use Step 1 regularly, you'll discover that you're prone to recurring states of mind, to repeating Locations with their distinctive Views and experiences of Reality. You need to notice and register these habitual states of mind as part of the Mapping process we spoke about earlier. In Step 1 you photograph them for your "recurring Location photo album." You note them as part of a kind of survey map in Step 1 so that you can return to them in Steps 4 and 5 to Map them in detail. This is the way you grow your self-knowledge about the forces at play in your life, knowledge that will become Steadfast Knowledge as you progress in your practice.

As you develop your awareness by using Step 1, you begin to see how often these habitual patterns dominate your life. These habitual patterns are your Self-Image and Briar Patch Locations. Someone can tell you that your basement is flooded until the end of time, but until you see it for yourself, or until you feel the wetness while standing in your own shoes—you really won't know for sure. You Map your territory through your own direct experience so that your knowledge will be reliable and valid.

Once you become directly aware of your Surface Identity and Self-Image based Locations, you'll see how their Views breed experiences of shaky uncertainty. The same holds true for discovering your Briar Patches Locations. As you practice Step 1 with dedication, you will notice that there are very sensitive spots within you that get triggered by particular situations. You'll begin to see this at first through the rear view mirror. Then you will grow able to notice things sooner; you'll realize that these sensitive spots are Briar Patch Locations that can swallow you up—unless you're aware.

One reason that we feel uncertain so often is that we are constantly shifting in and out of different states of mind. That might not be so troublesome if we didn't subscribe to the belief that we should always be one unchanging person. But after doing Step 1 for some time, you will make an important discovery. You'll discover that you live in a multi-family dwelling and not a single family home; you are not one single solid identity. There are many Locations within you, each with its own View and experience of Reality.

If you are to find Unshakable Certainty, you need to become familiar with these Locations and then learn how to host them rather than being defined or possessed by them. Instead of being swallowed up by fear and self-doubt, for example, you can then maintain your separation from them by remaining aware.

Step 1 helps us to establish awareness as a means of "Hosting" uncertainty based states of mind. Ultimately, you will discover awareness as your True Address and as the basis for Unshakable Certainty. It takes awhile to accomplish this, and perhaps like your first efforts to ride a bicycle, doing so may at first seem impossible. We learned to ride our bikes by continuing to make efforts, and once we discovered "balance" on the bike—we knew we could do it. Similarly, if you keep practicing Step 1, not only is it possible to find Unshakable Certainty—it's inevitable.

Step 2 in the Unshakable Certainty Process™ focuses on how we can support and strengthen the awareness that Step 1 gives us. In Step 2, we use the breath to deepen our awareness and stay awake. Let's turn to it now.

CHAPTER 3

The Unshakable Certainty Process™

STEP 2

Can I Breathe Free?

"WHEN WE EXHALE, WE RELEASE CARBON DIOXIDE, TENSION, AND STRESS. ...BREATHING QUIETS THE MIND, REDUCES BLOOD PRESSURE, UPLIFTS UNHEALTHY ATTITUDES, AND DECREASES PSYCHOSOMATIC SYMPTOMS."

—DR. CARON GOODE

"THE EFFECTS OF BREATHING EXTEND TO ... THE SUBTLE PHYSIOLOGICAL INTERACTIONS SUCH AS THE MOLECULAR PROCESSES THROUGH WHICH THE BODY'S ENERGY PRODUCTION IS MAINTAINED."

—ALAN HYMES, M.D.

"TOP ATHLETES SAY THAT WITHOUT BREATH AWARENESS, ALL OF THE STRENGTH AND FLEXIBILITY IN THE WORLD WON'T GET THEM TO THE FINISH LINE FIRST."

—NANCY COULTER-PARKER

THE UNSHAKABLE CERTAINTY PROCESS™

Step 1	Step 2	Step 3	Step 4	Step 5
L	B	R	I	C
Can I Locate Myself? Where Am I?	CAN I BREATHE FREE?	Can I Relocate?	Personify	Dialogue

STEP 2

In Step 2, we use the out breath in a special way to break free from any fixed Location and to connect to the calm, clear aware state of mind that is the foundation for the Free Position and for Unshakable Certainty.

To explain further, let me note a little background detail to give you a clear sense of what the "Free Breath" and "Breathing Free" is all about.

SOME BACKGROUND DETAIL ON STEP 2

I developed an early version of Step 2 while I was working with patients troubled by stress-related illnesses such as heart disease, high blood pressure, migraine and tension headaches and severe insomnia, to name just a few. I discovered that their illnesses were the result of their getting stuck in high stress Locations, Views and experiences of Reality.

They would get tuned to these Locations like your radio gets tuned to a particular station, and it plays the exclusive broadcast frequencies associated with that station. If your radio was tuned to a jazz station at 107.2, all you would hear was jazz; you wouldn't hear the talk show or the blues—unless you changed the station.

My patients would get stuck in Locations that were tuned to negative states of mind, such as fear, anxiety, self-doubt, worry and so on. They were stuck on a station that picked up only the energy frequencies of fear, worry and self-doubt story lines, story lines that triggered the release of illness causing stress hormones such as cortisol and epinephrine.

I taught hundreds of my patients the Breathing Free practice to teach them to change the station.

To understand just how a special out breath can do this, let's take a brief look at how the mindbody functions.

THE MINDBODY AND THE FREE BREATH

Your mind and body are not two separate things; they are an interdependent unit—the mindbody. What you think and feel manifests in your body every moment. And what goes on in your body affects what you think and feel.

In Step 2 in the Unshakable Certainty Process™ you use this knowledge to separate from a Location that broadcasts "uncertainty frequencies." Like a radio, when you're in a particular Location, your thoughts and feelings are in accord with the View and experience of Reality determined and defined by that station. If you are in a fear Location, for example, then the View and the Reality will generate fear-based thoughts and feelings. If you get stuck in that state of mind, its story lines will drive you deeper and deeper into uncertainty.

Step 2 delivers you to calm and clear freestanding awareness, awareness you can tune yourself to very easily. You ask yourself: Can I Breathe Free? As with Step 1, the question is really a prompt to action. It's in the form of a question to give you the complete feeling of control. It's your choice to do it; you're not following orders.

The action you take in Step 2 is a special use of the breath. You breathe free of any Location and tune yourself to the calm and clear awareness you find at the end of a Free Breath. Let's look over the instructions below, and as we go over them, you can do Step 2 to experience it yourself now.

HERE'S HOW WE DO STEP 2

- Take a deep in breath for about 3-4 seconds.
  — Your tummy should fill with air and expand.
- Hold your breath for a count of 1-2.
- Then—on the out breath—just <u>let go and release completely.</u>
  — That is, on the out breath—don't walk the breath out—allow it to release freely all at once.
- Tune yourself to the calm, clear, relaxed state of awareness that's at the end of the out breath.

This is the way to do Step 2 when you are alone and when drawing attention to yourself is not a problem. This is the best way to practice. As you develop your capacity to find the calm, clear state of awareness, then you can do a quiet and simple version of this Step in public with the same results.

My yellow lab dog companion, Tashi, does a variation of this out breath often. She'll be lying down, and then she relaxes completely with a deep out breath that sounds like a loud whisper. When you're alone practicing Step 2, it can help to give voice to the Free Breath as a good sigh, Hhhaaaaa!

Don't worry; in public you can drop any sound on the exhalation—it's not necessary. In time, you can do a version of this Free Breath anywhere, even while you're in the midst of a discussion with someone, without drawing any attention to yourself. I do Step 2 many times in the middle of talks I am giving to 600 people and more.

LET'S DO STEP 2 NOW

OK let's do Step 2 now. (If you can, add the voice as a sigh to it; if not, no need.)

- Take an in breath, hold briefly and then *completely let go* on the out breath.

Note how you feel. We'll do it again, this time focus sharply on the experience at the very end of the out breath, in the space between the out breath and the next in breath. Make sure to keep your mind with the out breath; don't let it wander around elsewhere. If your mind wanders, then you're just breathing, you're not tuning in to doing Step 2.

- Do another Free Breath now.

Let go and release completely; do so with your mind as well as your breath. Don't cling or hold on to any image, thought or feeling. Let your mind notice the relaxed state of calm, clear awareness that's at the end of your breathing out. You first meet this calm state by noticing how good it feels. Then in time, you can realize that the experience at the end of the out breath is a special experience. It's a calm, clear aware state of mind that you can train yourself to find, especially when you need to wake up and break free of any Location, View and Reality that's causing you shaky uncertainty. Let's do Step 2 again now.

- Take another Free Breath. This time really tune yourself to the state of mind at the end of the out breath.

This "tuning yourself" to the calm aware state is the way to train for finding Unshakable Certainty—it's the essence of what Step 2 is all about. You tune yourself to the aware state of mind, and you nurture and deepen it so that it ultimately becomes your Location, View and Reality. As we shall see, the awareness at the end of your special out breath is the precursor to the Free Position and to finding your True Address. As your connection to this state of mind becomes steady and stable, your View will grow more open and free, and your experience of Reality will grow more joyful and self-assured. In time you'll realize that all situations are workable, if you are aware. This is the Lion's Roar of complete self-assurance and the territory of Unshakable Certainty.

THE OUT BREATH IS THE MEANS— THE END IS THE CALM, AWARE STATE

At first you can easily lose your connection to the calm, aware state. While it's only another out breath away, you need to keep in mind that your breath is just the vehicle, it's not the destination. The calm and aware state of mind is the Step 2 destination. The out breath is just a means to get there. So, as you train using Step 2, do the following:

- Do a Free Breath to find the calm state of mind, and then just be in it as long as you can.
- When you lose it, do another out breath.
- When you lose it again, see if you can find the state without doing another out breath.
- Train to develop your capacity to stay in the state as deeply and as long as possible—that's the key to this Step in the Process.

The more you develop your capacity to find and rest in the calm state, the more you'll be able to use Step 2 when you need to break free from a Location that's dragging you into a Waking Dream, especially one inhabited by uncertainty monsters. Step 2 is like a bridge from your Wrong Address to your True Address. You move from a stressful Waking Dream populated with "shaky uncertainty monsters" to the calm, clear state and then on into the Free Position and Aware Presence.

We take an average of 22,000 breaths a day. If you can be in the state of awareness for just one percent of them, you'll experience deep and profound self-assurance, confidence and well-being as a result. The point for now is to become familiar enough with the calm, clear and aware state so that you can find it at will, an accomplishment that will allow you to Breathe Free of any troublesome state of mind.

MAKE THE CALM, CLEAR, AWARE STATE YOUR FRIEND

In time, the relaxed aware state will deepen and become like your friend, a friend who you've gotten to know very well, so well that you can recognize her anywhere. You know how to find her, and when you want to connect to her you can.

If you can find the aware state without using the out breath, that's fine. But you can always use the Free Breath as a bridge to break free from Waking Dreams and to connect to Unshakable Certainty.

Let's look again at the mindbody to better understand what gives Step 2 its power.

HOW STEP 2 CHANGES THE MINDBODY TO SUPPORT THE FREE POSITION

Recall that when you're caught in a Waking Dream being chased around by uncertainty monsters such as fear, self-doubt, insecurity and hesitation, it's as if you're stuck on a radio station that's announcing bad news based on false information. We can use Step 2, "Can I Breathe Free?" to change the radio station. We can do this because breathing not only moves air around—breathing also regulates the flow of energy within our mindbody.

Recall too that the mindbody is an interdependent unit, and so what we think and feel affects our body and what's going on in our body affects what we think and feel. By using a Free Breath to change what's going on in your body, you enable your mind to do two things:

- Break free from fixed and inflexible Waking Dream Locations, Views and Realities that breed shaky uncertainty, and

- wake up into calm, clear, awareness—awareness that will grow into the ultimate foundation for Unshakable Certainty.

Let's take a closer look at how this happens.

UNSHAKABLE CERTAINTY AND UNCERTAINTY ARE MINDBODY EVENTS

There are two switches on your nervous system that lie outside of your conscious control.

1. One is for emergencies; the emergency switch triggers the stress hormones that are part of the fight or flight response if you are in danger.

2. The other switch is the ordinary housekeeping switch; it's for taking care of your body's business and for calling forth your body's resources to renew, restore and heal itself.

When one switch is "on", the other is off.

<u>Step 2, "Can I Breathe Free?" is so powerful because the Free Breath shuts down the emergency switch and shaky uncertainty and turns on the well-being switch and the foundation for Unshakable Certainty.</u>

Shaky uncertainty is a mindbody event. When you feel fear, self-doubt and insecurity, and when you fall into them as a Waking Dream, your body cannot tell the difference between your Waking Dream experience of danger and actual danger. For example, it cannot tell the difference between your fears and worries about financial disaster and actual financial disaster.

As a result, when you feel fear and uncertainty, your body can trigger the emergency switch and signal your inner pharmacy to release stress hormones to prepare you for fight or flight. This unnecessary release of stress hormones does more than just threaten your health.

It also locks you into a fixed Location, View and Reality (as if you're on a particular radio station) of shaky uncertainty. The resulting stress hormones make you vigilant and put you into a survival mode where you pick up signs inside and outside of yourself that reinforce your fear and self-doubt. Step 2, "Can I Breathe Free?" is not only great for your body; it also enables your mind to break free from any Location that has a hold on it.

The state of calm awareness liberates you from any fixed position. As you deepen and steady your connection to this state, you can Relocate to a deeper version of it, the Free Position (Step 3 up ahead). When you can remain connected to the calm, clear, aware state, then your mindbody is in a position that supports Unshakable Certainty.

STEP 2 IS A BRIDGE CONNECTING STEPS 1 AND 3

Let's sum up. Step 1 gives us a quick wake-up call. We ask: "Can I Locate Myself?" "Where Am I?" and immediately a sliver of awareness breaks off and sees where we are and what's going on. Sometimes this sliver of awareness becomes stable and can free us, but because of the power of the mindbody connection, the Waking Dream we're stuck in can shut down that sliver of awareness. This happens especially with Locations that have deep roots and a long history—such as our Self-Image or our Briar Patches.

Your Self-Image and Briar Patches are wired into your mindbody. They are like the radio stations we mentioned earlier; when you're in any of these Locations you pick up the broadcast frequencies of their Views and the experiences of Reality defined by those Views. Your conditioned Self-Image and your Briar Patches are like powerful 500,000-watt stations whose power dominates the airwaves of what you think and feel. It's hard to get far enough out of their range to break free from them and tune into something else, into more of who you truly are.

That's why Step 2 is so important. You use it to Breathe Free of the Location, no matter how powerful it is, before it has a chance to suck you back in. The calm, clear, aware state of mind is like a rescue helicopter that swoops down and takes you out of stormy seas. Step 2 is a bridge that takes you away from uncertainty-based Waking Dreams; it also allows you to find, steady and stabilize the calm, clear, aware state so that you can Relocate to the Free Position in Step 3.

Experienced practitioners of the Process often do Steps 1, 2 and 3 in an instant—so close together that they can't really tell them apart. Again, once you really learn the first three Steps of the UC Process™, they will come together as one smooth and graceful dance. Practice to make it so.

Let's now turn to Step 3 of the Unshakable Certainty Process™; it's our final destination. When we can Relocate to the Free Position and Aware Presence, we've not only found Unshakable Certainty, we can begin to live from it.

CHAPTER 4

The Unshakable Certainty Process™

STEP 3

Can I Relocate?

"I KNOW BUT ONE FREEDOM AND THAT IS THE
FREEDOM OF THE MIND."
—ANTOINE DE SAINT-EXUPERY

"NO MAN IS FREE WHO IS NOT MASTER OF HIMSELF."
—EPICTETUS

"FREEDOM IS NOT BEING A SLAVE
TO ANY CIRCUMSTANCE."
—SENECA

"THE LAST OF THE HUMAN FREEDOMS IS
TO CHOOSE ONE'S ATTITUDES."
—VICTOR FRANKL

THE UNSHAKABLE CERTAINTY PROCESS™

Step 1	Step 2	Step 3	Step 4	Step 5
Can I Locate Myself? Where Am I?	Can I Breathe Free?	CAN I RELOCATE?	Personify	Dialogue

STEP 3

In Step 2 of the Unshakable Certainty Process™, we found the calm, clear, aware state of mind; in Step 3 <u>we Relocate there</u>.

In Step 3, we deepen and steady our experience of that state of mind as the Free Position, and then we increasingly take up residence there with benefit of its open View and flexible experience of Reality.

The Free Position is a state of mind that allows us to stand open, aware and free, free from the literal story line in any LVR that might breed fear, self-doubt and insecurity. This state is our connection to our True Address, Aware Presence. Aware Presence gives us the ability to be awake—here and now; <u>it's the key to Unshakable Certainty.</u>

Following find a graphic representation that sums up where we Relocate from and where we Relocate to.

WRONG ADDRESS	**TRUE ADDRESS**
Surface Identity	Innermost Identity
Self-Image and Briar Patches	Calm, Clear, Aware State of Mind
Unconscious and conditioned Locations with fixed literal Views and inflexible experiences of Reality	Conscious Location as the Free Position with open View and Flexible experience of Reality
Identified with and possessed by any state of mind as the one true LVR	Unidentified, awareness based "Hosting" of any state of mind as one LVR among others
Waking Dreams fueled by thoughts and feelings about the past and the future	Aware Presence Now
Shaky uncertainty	Unshakable Certainty

HOW TO DO STEP 3 OF THE PROCESS

Let's briefly review Steps 1 and 2 so that we can see Step 3 against a crystal clear background. And keep in mind that in time these three Steps will come together as a fluid, smooth dance.

STEP 1 REVIEWED

In Step 1 you ask: Can I Locate Myself? Where am I? This is your wake-up call. Before you did Step 1, you were as if in a dream without knowing it.

Step 1 frees up a sliver of awareness that becomes aware of

your state of mind for what it is—a Location, View and Reality (LVR).

STEP 2 REVIEWED

Then you do Step 2 of the Process. You ask: Can I Breathe Free? You Breathe Free by taking one or more Free Breaths. This special out breath loosens the mindbody grip that the fear and self-doubt Location has on you.

At the same time, you tune yourself to the calm, clear state of awareness that's at the end of the special out breath. If need be, you do this a few times to really establish your connection to this relaxed, aware state.

In Step 2, you Breathe Free from the narrow, fixed and inflexible fear and self-doubt Location, and you train to move into the open, free and flexible Location of the clear, calm, aware state of mind.

STEP 3

Now in Step 3 you ask: Can I Relocate? Can I steady my connection to this free and flexible Location so that I can take up residence in it as the Free Position, as my True Address and as the basis of Unshakable Certainty? That's the question and the essence of Step 3.

To do this, you must not only develop the capacity to find and steady yourself in the Free Position, but also commit yourself to doing what it takes to stay awake as well. The commitment issue is both a short and long-term one. In the short-term you face it during your initial and ongoing practice of Step 2, Can I Breathe Free?

At the end of the Free Breath, your mind has a natural tendency to return to the surface noise. Your mind experiences something of the calm, clear, aware state, but then it falls back into surface drama of the Waking Dream. This is exactly like waking up from a sleeping dream, but before you have the chance to fully awaken from the dream— you fall asleep and back into it again.

But in Step 3, instead of being willing to fall back into the surface drama, you <u>commit</u> on the spot to remain in the aware state. Your commitment becomes your willingness to find and Relocate to the Free Position as your gold standard for your quality of life. Step 3 is a decision point of sorts. You decide to marry awareness, as you're beyond just dating. Seeing what's at stake, you choose awareness as a life partner.

In the longer term, the commitment that Step 3 asks for in the question: "Can I Relocate?" is for us to realize the value of being awake and to choose it, to commit to it as a way of life. It's a commitment to Relocate from our Wrong Address to our True Address—and to live from there.

As you steady your connection to the calm, clear, aware state of mind, and as you commit to it, you move more deeply into the Free Position. You not only can find the Free Position now, but you can Relocate to it and reside in it. The Free Position now becomes an Aware Presence that you embody, an Aware Presence that is beyond getting caught up in narrow and conditioned Locations with fixed Views and experiences of Reality plagued by uncertainty.

This Aware Presence is wide awake; it's a Location-less Location with a completely wide open View and a flexible experience of Reality. It has no agenda or attachments whatsoever. It just is. You discover that it is a joy to just be awake and present here and now. Aware Presence is where you belong; you've returned home.

Like a still pond on a well-lighted full moon night, the

Aware Presence of your Innermost Identity is a consciousness that reflects the moon, clouds and geese flying over, but it isn't touched, changed or moved by them.

In Step 3, you cultivate and then Relocate to an Aware Presence as a consciousness that reflects the fear, self-doubt and insecurity of shaky uncertainty without ever being touched, changed or moved by them. Fears, doubts, worries and so on still come up, but you realize that you are separate from them. They no longer drag you into uncertainty. The Free Position and Aware Presence are the two sides of the same Unshakable Certainty coin. Unshakable Certainty is none other than a deep and stable awareness that allows you to "accurately see," "understand" and "handle" what is going on inside and outside of you—right now.

Unshakable Certainty is your True Address. But you need to find it before you can claim it, and then you need to do the work needed to be able to actually take up residence there. That's what Steps 4 and 5 of the Process are all about. Let's turn to them now.

CHAPTER 5

The Unshakable Certainty Process™

Steps 4 and 5:

Personify and Dialogue

"...A TRAUMATIC WOUNDING BRINGS ABOUT A DISSOCIATION OF PART OF THE PSYCHE WHICH IS THEN NO LONGER CONSCIOUS OR UNDER CONSCIOUS CONTROL. ... EVERYTHING MUST BE DONE TO HELP THE UNCONSCIOUS TO REACH THE CONSCIOUS MIND AND BE FREE FROM ITS RIGIDITY. "

—JUNG

"...WHAT IS NOT ADMITTED INTO AWARENESS ERUPTS IN ... OBSESSIVE, LITERALISTIC WAYS, AFFLICTING CONSCIOUSNESS WITH PRECISELY THE QUALITIES IT STRIVES TO EXCLUDE."

—JAMES HILLMAN

"WE MUST BECOME ACQUAINTED WITH OUR EMOTIONAL HOUSE-HOLD: WE MUST SEE OUR FEELINGS AS THEY ACTUALLY ARE. THIS BREAKS THEIR HYPNOTIC AND DAMAGING HOLD ON US."

—VERNON HOWARD

THE UNSHAKABLE CERTAINTY PROCESS™

Step 1	Step 2	Step 3	Step 4	Step 5
Can I Locate Myself? Where Am I?	Can I Breathe Free?	Can I Relocate?	PERSONIFY	DIALOGUE

STEPS 4 AND 5 PERSPECTIVE

In Steps 1-3 of the Unshakable Certainty Process™, we first break free from the Locations that trigger our Waking Dreams and we find and cultivate the clear, calm, aware state. Then we move on to the Free Position and we Relocate to Aware Presence, to the ultimate seat of Unshakable Certainty.

In Step 4, Personify, and Step 5, Dialogue, we do the work needed to place that seat on reliable ground. These two sequential Steps work to create the inner foundation we need to live from deep conviction and extraordinary self-assurance.

Steps 4 and 5 are <u>indispensable</u>. Steps 1-3 will deliver you to Aware Presence, but you won't be able to maintain a strong connection to it. You'll lose the connection because your conditioning and your Briar Patches will inevitably pull you out of alignment with your Innermost Identity. Steps 4 and 5 allow you to Map and modify your conditioned patterns and your Briar Patches so that you can put them in perspective and manage or eliminate them.

Let's take a brief look at the Steps now. Then we'll examine what they do and how, and then we'll learn how to do them properly.

PERSONIFY AND DIALOGUE

In Step 4, you use your Imagination to Personify a Location as if it was a separate personality. When you Personify a state of mind, you represent and portray that state of mind as a separate character.

Then in Step 5, you communicate with that personified personality in Dialogue form—you have a meaningful conversation with it—so you can learn about its View and its Reality. As you use Steps 4 and 5 to gain knowledge about your conditioned and Briar Patch states of mind, you grow the Steadfast Knowledge you need to redefine, eliminate or manage these conditioned patterns and past hurts so that you can be more emotionally even and so less troubled by uncertainty.

WHAT STEPS 4 AND 5 DO—AND HOW

When you Map the View and Reality of a Briar Patch, or of your conditioned Self-Image, you develop the eyes to see and modify the forces that drive your feelings and thoughts, especially the forces that drive them into shaky uncertainty. You can't become free until and unless you have the knowledge of what to become free from. Steps 4 and 5 give you that knowledge. The following brief analogy points to the relationship between knowledge and freedom.

If you deeply know and understand that the earth is not flat and that strong winds are caused by weather conditions and not because God is angry with you, then when a hurricane comes, you don't have to be afraid that God is trying to blow you off the face of the earth because you are bad.

Similarly, if you know through direct experience that your feelings, thoughts and actions based on fear, self-doubt and insecurity arise from your Briar Patch wounds and from your conditioning, then you KNOW that experiences of uncertainty do not mean that you are truly in danger or that you are less than you should be or need to be. When your knowing becomes steadfast, then your knowledge itself becomes freedom.

Steps 4 and 5 are necessary because if you never really learn about or deal with the causes of your fear, self-doubt and insecurity, you're only deceiving yourself by trying to bypass your uncertainty rather than undoing it. You can't achieve Unshakable Certainty unless you put your inner house in order.

DO STEPS 4 AND 5 WITH JOYFUL EFFORT

It's not always easy work to put our inner house in order, but it doesn't have to be heavy handed serious work that's a Big Deal struggle. If we keep the View from Aware Presence in mind, we can do Steps 4 and 5 with joyful effort.

At the end of the last chapter, we noted that Aware Presence is inherently pleasurable and satisfying; put simply, it feels very good to be awake. The View from Aware Presence is calm, open, radiant and because it's not attached to outcomes or agendas of any kind—utterly free. Just a few minutes in this boundless View will lighten your load and brighten your feeling and thought with open-hearted self-assurance.

Train to practice Steps 4 and 5 from the View of Aware Presence, or at least from the calm state, because when you Map your conditioning and your Briar Patches, your ordinary mind will have to see what it doesn't want to know about itself. You'll be traveling through earlier time zones in your psyche, and some of them are bound to be temporarily uncomfortable.

If you find yourself getting too identified with a Briar Patch, immediately refresh your awareness by doing Steps 1-3; that way you can let go of any troublesome state of mind. Then, once refreshed, you can return to Map a Briar Patch from the Free Position instead of an identified one. Advanced practitioners of the Process effortlessly refresh, enhance and strengthen their Aware Presence as needed during their day. You can begin to do the same—just stay alert and do the practice.

It's also a good idea to bring your sense of humor along. When you're Mapping your Briar Patches and your conditioning, you need to be able to laugh at yourself so you can appreciate your share of how absurd and crazy the human dilemma can be at times. A warm-hearted sense of humor is a cardinal sign of the emotional intelligence that comes with awareness, and it's part of the wealth that comes with Unshakable Certainty.

You don't want to use Steps 4 and 5 in a grim atmosphere when your mood is deadly serious. If you work from the View of the Free Position, and if you keep the dots connected and your eyes on the prize of Unshakable Certainty, your inner work will be like that of a gardener. You'll be like a gardener who can work joyfully to prepare the spring soil because she already smells the sweet scent of the summer flowers that will follow her labors.

Now let's turn to the heart of what makes Steps 4 and 5 remarkable.

SEPARATION AND HOSTING

The essential premise of Steps 4 and 5 is a paradox. It's as follows:

You can only stay separate from and host a troublesome Location if you connect and relate to it.

This premise is critical to your inner work. On the one hand, when your conditioning or your Briar Patches lie dormant, you are unaware of them; it's as if they don't exist. On the other hand, when they're triggered and active, you become them. That is, their Views overtake you and define your Reality—without your realizing it. In either case, you can't get enough separation to see what's happening, and so you can't do anything about it. You're essentially helpless.

Steps 4 and 5 allow you to gain separation through connecting and relating to your conditioning and Briar Patches, and so these Steps empower you to see what's going on, and to host troublesome states of mind instead of becoming possessed by them.

STEPS 4 AND 5 ILLUSTRATED

Always do Steps 4 and 5 together in sequence, either following Steps 1-3 or at a later time. Let's use an illustration to put using the Steps into concrete focus so we can proceed with clarity. Imagine that you wake up one day frightened, insecure and depressed. Perhaps a sleeping dream delivered you to this state of mind; a state of mind that is now driving you into a Waking Dream focused on depression.

Imagine too that the depressed Location is just sitting right on top of you—you're identified with its View and Reality. You feel sad, lonely and hopeless. Then imagine the following:

*   Something in you remembers the Process and you do Step 1. You ask: "Where Am I?" A sliver of awareness breaks off and you align yourself with that sliver of awareness instead of with the depression Location.

*   After taking a mental photo of the Location, you do Step 2 of the Process—you Breathe Free of its View and Reality and rest in the calm state of mind.

*   Then you do Step 3 and Relocate to the Free Position and to Aware Presence.

Clearly, Steps 1-3 are a move into greater awareness. You transcend or move beyond the limits and boundaries of the Location you were caught in, but there's a problem if you leave it at that. If we could give your depression a microphone, it would ask,

"Wait, where you going? What about me?" In transcending your depressed state of mind, you've also abandoned it on some level.

Steps 4, Personify, and 5, Dialogue of the Process protect you from trying to bypass what's in the way of your making a stable connection to Unshakable Certainty. Let's continue our illustration to see what these two Steps are all about and what they will do for you.

So, imagine that you are now using Steps 4 and 5 to connect to your depressed state of mind so you can relate to it, and so it won't possess you with its fixed Views. By personifying it as a separate character, you can now treat it as a guest, as an invisible guest.

You can't learn anything from a state of mind that's sitting on top of you, but you can learn a lot from a "visiting guest." By engaging your depression in "meaningful conversation," you open up a channel of communication within yourself for self-knowledge that could not be opened otherwise. You gain access to parts of yourself that are usually walled off from your awareness. Steps 4 and 5 put you in a position to ask important questions, questions such as: "Who or what is this depression? And what does it want from me? Does it need to tell me something? Where does it come from?" Your invisible guest can answer these questions and tell you about its Views, and it can give clear voice to its message and meaning.

Using Steps 4 and 5, you learn to be <u>with</u> a state of mind— not <u>in</u> it (identified with it). As we saw, this trains you to be able to host Locations rather than becoming possessed by them. Step 5, Dialogue, allows you to hear directly from your depression about its concerns. This exchange of ideas between your conscious stance and parts of yourself, parts that are usually unknown to you, feeds and grows your Steadfast Knowledge.

Your Steadfast Knowledge will help you to heal, grow and awaken—and so establish the inner conditions for Unshakable Certainty.

The literal View of your depressed Location could be that things are bad, that you are not enough and so on. This View defines your Reality as hopeless and it leaves you feeling helpless. But when you Personify and then Dialogue with your depressed Location, it can open up so you can hear a deeper message, a message from your Innermost Identity—one with a deeper View and so a different Reality.

Its deeper View could be that you are living too much at the surface of life; perhaps because of your Briar Patch-based fears of failure and so on. You could discover that your depression is a message about Briar Patch wounds that you need to face and heal, or that it symbolizes the fact that you're not honoring the life that you truly want and need to live because you're confined by your conditioned Self-Image.

All of these deeper meanings often lie coded in the surface Views of the troublesome states of mind we regularly experience. Because these deeper messages fly beneath our radar, we miss them and so we miss appreciating what's really going on in our lives. Steps 4 and 5 change all that.

SAFEGUARD'S INITIAL RESISTANCE

At first, Safeguard won't know exactly why you are using Steps 4 and 5, and he may get ticked off when you try to open the doors he's worked so hard to keep shut. Because he's stuck in past time, his View of the situation may be that you're heading for danger, not for Unshakable Certainty. Only by growing your Steadfast Knowledge will you be able to re-educate Safeguard, and bring him into present time so he can see and protect your real-time interests.

Recall that Safeguard's one aim is your survival; he knows nothing about helping you to live well. He wants to keep you separate from those past time wounds that he mistakenly regards as a threat in present time. He needs to wake up to the fact you're your real-time concerns are focused on creating the inner conditions that will align your feelings, thoughts and actions with your True Address and Unshakable Certainty.

Uneducated Safeguard also mistakes your Wrong Address for your one and only home. He wants to hold onto it for dear life, because it's the only one he knows. He knows nothing of your True Address, of your Innermost Identity. Steps 4 and 5 will grow your Steadfast Knowledge so you can gradually introduce Safeguard to your real home and awaken him to the difference between life lived from surface-based Waking Dreams and life lived from the depths of Unshakable Certainty.

You should expect some resistance from Safeguard; he may try to discourage your efforts. Be alert, because he'll whisper something like what follows in your ear to throw you off track:

"This Dialoguing is stupid, it's not gonna lead anywhere. Let's stop and do something else."

Again, be aware; don't let him trick you into not practicing. Do so with joyful effort and with the big picture in mind. Once Safeguard awakens to what Steadfast Knowledge knows, you'll be home free.

A NOTE OF CARE AND GOOD SENSE

As noted at the outset of Chapter 2, the Process is best learned and practiced with expert instruction and supervision.

This is especially the case for Steps 4 and 5 because they involve work with our Briar Patches and our family-based conditioning. If you have a history of psychological problems, or if you have been through a lot of trauma and turmoil in your life, then you should not use these Steps without expert guidance and support.

ON WORKING WITH THE IMAGINATION IN STEPS 4 AND 5

The creative Imagination is a powerful resource for doing life-changing inner work. In 30 years of helping people connect to and live from who they deeply are, I've found that the Imagination offers unmatched openings for creating the inner conditions we need to support Unshakable Certainty.

Too often people use their conceptual minds to speculate about the nature and the sources of their conditioning and about their Briar Patch-related problems. In doing so, they generate a lot of rational sounding ideas to try to figure out what's going on. This can be useful, but it's often a dead end filled with a pile of notions, memories and theories that don't really change too much of anything, if anything at all.

Conceptual ideas have their place, but they can't really penetrate or change our conditioning or our Briar Patch wounds. The Imagination can. That's why it's such a powerful resource for deep inner work and for growing Steadfast Knowledge.

If you're not accustomed to working with your Imagination, Steps 4 and 5 may seem a little weird, and Dialoguing with a personified invisible guest may feel silly, awkward and of questionable value to you. I sometimes still feel strange when I begin a Dialogue and it may take me five or ten minutes to open things up. If you can persist with a light touch and with your eye on the prize of Unshakable Certainty, then you'll soon discover why these Steps are so powerful.

You'll discover that trying to explore a state of mind without these tools is like trying to pick up a board you're standing on. It can't be done, at least not deeply and thoroughly. By imagining a state of mind as a distinct personality, you get the separation you need to pick the board up and see what it feels like, and you get to discover what lies underneath it.

Moreover, the truth is that you have many inner faces. There are many different Locations within you, but because you assume you are one identity with a single face, you miss a lot that's going on in your life. When you Personify a Location and then Dialogue with it—you have a chance to get to know and honor the different parts of yourself, parts that often seem so different that they can create confusion and uncertainty, sometimes on a daily basis.

THE POWER OF THE CREATIVE IMAGINATION—SOME EXAMPLES

Let's look together at a few examples of the power of our creative Imagination.

As noted earlier, in my many years of work with therapy patients, consulting clients and meditation students, I have never found a more effective tool for deep inner work and profound personal growth. I used early forms of the Imagination-based Steps 4 and 5 while working with people troubled by varying degrees of depression. When they Personified and Dialogued with their depression, they often learned exactly why they were depressed and what to do about it. Their depression taught them pretty much everything they needed to know and do.

Most stopped taking medication because there was no need

for it. And many learned that their depression was not a symptom of an illness—it was really more like a message that they needed to understand. The message was that something deep inside of them was not living the life it needed to; the message needed to be recognized and honored, not medicated.

When our Innermost Identity doesn't get what it needs, it suffers like a plant that doesn't get enough sun and water. Depression is often the suffering that happens to people who are living too much from their Surface Identity, from their Wrong Address. By Personifying and Dialoguing with a depression, or with any Location, we get to hear its story in its own voice.

The work of great writers and actors give us another example of the Imagination's power. They regularly use the creative Imagination to dive deep into an imagined character via their own real feelings to illuminate and explore the powerful forces that are the real source of events at the surface of life.

You can feel the power of the Imagination by doing the following exercise right now. Read all of the following bulleted instructions first and then do it.

- Close your eyes and take a deep in breath and do an out breath as in Step 2.
- Then in your mind's eye imagine a bright yellow lemon, a lemon that you slice in half.
- Pick the lemon up in your right hand. Feel its weight and texture.
- Now open your mouth, stick your tongue out, and squeeze some lemon juice on your tongue.
- Allow yourself to fully experience the taste and the sensations of the lemon juice dripping onto your tongue.

As simple as this lemon exercise is, it illustrates the power of your "mind's eye." There was no physical lemon that your eyes could see, no physical lemon that your hand could feel, no physical lemon juice that your tongue could taste. Despite this, you saw and felt a lemon and you tasted lemon juice. With other words, your Imagination gave you experiential knowledge. Similarly, when you can imagine a state of mind such as fear, worry or depression as a separate personality—you can develop experiential knowledge of what that state of mind is all about.

Let's turn now to look at some important procedures and guidelines for using Steps 4 and 5.

CONNECTING TO YOUR IMAGINATION

Some practitioners learn Steps 1-3 quickly and easily, but they have difficulty with Steps 4 and 5, whereas others have trouble with Steps 1-3, but they get Steps 4 and 5 right away.

Your experience with Steps 4 and 5 will depend on your relationship with your Imagination. If you haven't used it a great deal, if you're a stranger to the power of your mind's eye, then it may take you a little longer to get the hang of things. If, instead, you have a good connection to your Imagination, then you could be Dialoguing with a Personified Briar Patch within 30 minutes. Oh boy! Just be patient and plan on getting expert instruction and guidance if you feel confused.

One way of sharpening your imaginal skills is to just awaken to how important a role the Imagination plays in our lives. Children are great at using theirs. They can play house for two hours with a big cardboard box and a few pillows and two or three toys. Did you use your Imagination as a child? If so, remember how you did and what it felt like.

Think too of the songs that really move you. The lyrics and music come together in images that bring tears to your eyes while you recall a time or a person that meant so much to you. The powerful emotions you feel are the result of the interplay of your Imagination and those of the songwriter and singer.

What are your favorite films? Think of them and then realize that the entire film—the dialogue, the scenery, the music—was all the work of the Imagination.

And finally, just reflect on your dreams. Perhaps you can recall one that was especially powerful. Dreams are pure Imagination. The images in your dreams offer you a connection to something inside of you, something that the images represent and correspond to.

PROCEDURES AND PRINCIPLES FOR DOING STEPS 4 AND 5

You can do Steps 4 and 5 as follows. Put your inner work face on—the one connected to the View of Aware Presence and the Free Position, or at least to the calm state. And remember to approach Steps 4 and 5 with joyful effort and with a sense of humor about the human dilemma. Take a seat that's comfortable and sit with pen and paper in hand (or you can record the Dialogue, or do it at a computer). When possible, keep a record of your Dialogues, one you can use for reference and as a resource if you work with an expert guide.

Then Personify the Location you want to work as a separate character, and then give that character a name (e.g. Grumpy, Insecure Me, Mr. Guilt). Let the personified character you have created sit across from you, as if he or she was actually there. You don't need to see or visualize the character you've personified, just feel their presence and improvise as if you were sitting talking to an invisible guest. You can speak out loud or silently—whichever you prefer. You can "speak" out loud for your personified character spontaneously or you can listen with your inner ear to "hear" and record what he or she has to say. Be experimental—don't make a Big Deal out of things. Practice with a light touch and follow the approach that works best for you.

Although there are many different stances you can take in a Dialogue, it may be easiest for you to begin with an "Interviewer Stance," one where you could just ask questions. Once you learn the Steps, then you can try other Dialogue roles for yourself. In any case, write down as accurately as possible what you say and what the personified character says. The written or recorded Dialogue becomes part of your self-knowledge and Mapping base. Let's summarize this sequence as follows:

- Establish a mood of joyful effort and self-acceptance—with sense of humor intact.
- Locate yourself.
- Breathe Free.
- Establish yourself in calm state or in the Free Position.
- Use your creative Imagination to Personify and name the Location.
- Push gently through any awkwardness as resistance.
- Interview the Location as if it was a guest. Do so silently or in active voice, whatever you prefer.
- Flush out more of its View and Reality. Let the personified character speak silently or through your active voice, whatever works best for you.
- Write down or record the Dialogue.

You shouldn't try to program your Dialogues. This can be tricky at first because you may find yourself trying to "play the role" of a personified character. It's OK to prime the pump a little to get things going, but you need to give the characters you create in Step 4 the freedom to be who they are. They need to speak for themselves.

Your job is to host your them properly; don't try to dominate or control them. Remember to treat them as your guests. Steps 4 and 5 give you strong access to the inside of your Briar Patches and your conditioned states of mind. You want to uncover the hidden ideas, thoughts and feelings that make a Briar Patch tick—<u>from its own point of View.</u> The point is that when you Dialogue with a personality you create in Step 4, you must relate to that personality with respect. Or else it won't trust you. You might discover that a personified character is very young or very needy or very angry and so on. And so you must be aware enough to act accordingly in each situation.

With these guidelines in mind, let's move on now to a closer look at how to do Step 4.

AN ILLUSTRATION: HOW TO USE STEP 4

We can approach a clearer appreciation for Steps 4 and 5 by illustration. Imagine that I am Joe Schmidt, a guy stuck in a nasty guilt and self-doubt Location, View and Reality. Imagine also that I am so possessed by this state of mind that I just can't get a handle on it; I'm not sure what's going on.

It dawns on me that I feel this way a lot of the time.

I do Steps 1-3 of the Unshakable Certainty Process™ to break free of the Location and to Relocate to the Free Position. This works just fine for me—as long as I am aware and present in the Now. But when I am not, I notice that I often fall back into fear, guilt and self-doubt Waking Dreams, and it worries me. I sometimes get pretty depressed over it; I just don't know what to do to stop feeling uncertain about myself and as if I have done something bad or wrong. Using Steps 1-3, I seem to get rid of the Xerox copies of my guilt, but I just can't seem to get at the originals.

So I turn to my Imagination as an instrument that will allow me to connect with the originals and to grow my Steadfast Knowledge. I turn to Step 4 of the Process and I Personify and imagine my guilt as a separate being, as a distinct personality. I have a feel for him as a very angry guy who is real down on himself and filled with feelings of inadequacy and self-reproach. I name him Mr. Guilt.

Now that I've Personified this troublesome state of mind as Mr. Guilt, as a character separate from me, I can begin to turn to Step 5 to Dialogue with him. Mr. Guilt now represents the voice of the View and Reality of my guilt and self-doubt.

When I Personify my guilt and self-doubt Location as Mr. Guilt, I get enough separation from him to be with him, <u>without becoming him</u>. This is new and different. As noted earlier, when my guilt and self-doubt are not around, I am unaware of them, and when they do come around, they take me over completely—I become them. But now it's different—I have awareness and separation.

Through Step 4, I can now stand away from the guilty Views that Mr. Guilt represents. But, unlike in Steps 1-3, in Steps 4 and 5 I am not looking to break free from this troublesome state of mind, I am looking instead to Map it—to study it, to get to know it, to understand what it's all about.

Let's take a close look at how to do this with Step 5.

HOW TO USE STEP 5

In Step 5, I now Dialogue with the character I personified in Step 4, Mr. Guilt. I sit down on my sofa and I imagine Mr. Guilt across from me sitting in a chair. I decide to play the role of interviewer. I conduct the interview as a third party as if I was talking to Mr. Guilt about his feelings toward someone other than myself. I could fight with Mr. Guilt, but I decide to gather information as an interviewer to begin to Map things clearly. It's less provocative and easier for me to get my bearings this way.

I proceed to Dialogue with Mr. Guilt, in interview form, so I can flush out the View and Reality of this Location, and so I can better understand its source. The pieces of Dialogue below are real; they are selections from the Dialogues of someone who worked with me. We have his permission to examine them and we owe him a thank you.

Interviewer (I): Why do you give Joe such a hard time?

Mr. Guilt (MG): Because he's bad. He hurt his parents. He always hurts them. All he thinks about is himself. He breaks their hearts.

I: What do you mean? When? How?

MG: He just always hurts them. He says mean things to his father all the time and he treats his mother as if she was a maid.

I: Isn't that exactly what his mother says to him?

MG: Well she's right isn't she? She knows him better than anyone else. He makes her wait on him hand and foot. Even when she's tired, he comes in and he wants to eat. He makes her get up and cook for him.

As I become more experienced with the Dialoguing, I can bring in a third party. I can now enter the Dialogue as myself, as Upset Joe, as follows in this next excerpt:

Upset Joe (UJ): Now just a minute, that's bull. I come over to visit my mother and she insists on cooking. I don't even want eat, but I do it to please her.

MG: Oh come on UJ, you're lying, that's not true.

UJ: I am not lying you idiot. Don't tell me I'm lying. I don't lie. You're always on me. Get off of my back dammit.

As we Dialogue with our inner characters, something in us observes and consciously realizes what's going on, and we are changed as a result. For example, if I had no idea about the existence of Mr. Guilt, then when I fell into him as a Briar Patch Location, he would possess me with his point of View. And then I would feel guilty and regard Mr. Guilt's View and Reality as literally real.

By Personifying and Dialoguing with Mr. Guilt, I now learn that someone in me feels that way, someone who I don't have to agree with because I know that his Views are not literally true or accurate. <u>As a consequence, the Mr. Guilt Briar Patch becomes part of my conscious awareness, and as a result he loses political power within my personality</u>. He can no longer leave me feeling shaky and uncertain as much as he used to.

All of this now means that I am building a steadier foundation upon which to establish and maintain Aware Presence and Unshakable Certainty.

Briar Patches like Mr. Guilt and even characters such as Upset Joe can function as fragmentary parts within our personalities, fragmentary parts that are caught in past time. The house of our personality has many rooms, many Locations, and not all of them exist in the same time zone. Mr. Guilt may be a Briar Patch View that is very young. My adult mind may have moved beyond accepting any notion that I am always wrong. But Mr. Guilt may be a fragment of me from a younger age, one who felt so guilty that he was actually in danger as a result. And so Safeguard edited Mr. Guilt out of my consciousness.

But the boy inside of Mr. Guilt is stuck in the conviction that he is always wrong, and that he knows nothing of my knowledge to the contrary. My job is to help and heal the boy stuck in Mr. Guilt, not to flee from him, especially not try to flee from him into awareness.

Mr. Guilt still exists as a past time Location with a View and Reality that feels literal and compellingly real. And I am left shaky and uncertain from having to protect myself from him and by what happens to me when I fall into him as a Briar Patch. By entering into Dialogue with Mr. Guilt, my conscious mind begins to realize just how powerful the source of guilt is within my personality. And I can begin to go toward that little boy and heal him—because I now see Mr. Guilt for who he is.

I can now actually go back and rescue the boy inside of Mr. Guilt, take care of him, and bring him and Safeguard, who stands guard over him, into present time. This opens my heart and it deepens my connection to my Innermost Identity. Most importantly, it changes my psychology in ways that can better support Unshakable Certainty.

Because of my increasing self-knowledge, I am growing Steadfast Knowledge and she can now help me to have a

Dialogue of a deeper and different order, as seen in the following excerpt.

Mr. Guilt (MG): Joe, you're wrong for not calling your mother today; it's been over a week since she's heard from you. You don't really love her. You want to hurt her.

Aware Joe (AJ): No, I don't think so. I think that you never feel OK about just being free in your own life. If Mom wanted to talk to me, she can call me. I'm busy and I have tons of important things to do.

MG: Things that are more important than your mother?

AJ: That's silly. We don't have to weigh this or that against Mom and fear that she always has to be more important. It's true that what I am doing is very important to me. It's something I want a lot.

I think you never feel OK about just doing what you want to do. You always seem to feel that you've done something wrong or bad relating to Mom.

MG: I guess I do. I always have felt that way.

AJ: How's it feel?

MG: I feel worried and anxious a lot. As if she's gonna be upset and hurt, and that I am the cause of her pain. And I'm scared she'll be mad at me and not love me anymore.

AJ: MG, I feel bad for you. I want to help you feel more free and feel more OK just being in touch with what you feel and need, not what you think Mom feels and needs.

MG: I want you to help me do that. Yes, please help me.

This piece of Dialogue represents a more advanced connection between Joe and his Briar Patch, Mr. Guilt. That is, I now have good separation; I can host Mr. Guilt well. And the boy in Mr. Guilt feels received and cared for. Real communication is beginning to take place across different time zones. All of this feeds my Steadfast Knowledge tremendously. She can then better educate my Safeguard and bring him into present time. This is powerful inner work that dismantles the conditioning and the limitations that keep me stuck in my Wrong Address and in guilt, self-doubt and insecurity.

Most importantly, Steps 4 and 5 help me to build an authentic base in my life for Unshakable Certainty.

THE RIGHT ATTITUDE FOR USING STEPS 4 AND 5

One of the major obstacles to self-knowledge is the fact that we don't like ourselves; we regard our wounds and our conditioned limitations as weaknesses. I'm reminded of a comment the Dalai Lama made years ago. In response to a question about Westerners doing dedicated inner work on themselves, he said something that made a powerful impact on me. The Dalai Lama noted that he was amazed at the degree to which Westerners suffered from self-loathing. There was a moment of stunned silence in the room. Not because the comment was particularly shocking, but because those present knew all too well what he was talking about.

The fact is that you deserve to give yourself a break. And if you are to find and embody Unshakable Certainty, you need to treat yourself with love, respect and kindness. As the Buddha put it so well, "You, yourself, as much as anybody in the entire universe, deserve your love and affection."

To best use Steps 4 and 5, you need to cultivate an attitude of friendship and generosity toward yourself so that you can properly tend to and care for your inner life. To do this at high levels you must see your pain, self-doubt, problems and confusion as doors to self-knowledge and self-understanding—not as evidence that you're flawed as a person. Then and only then can you create the conditions to support Aware Presence and Unshakable Certainty.

The essence of Steps 4 and 5 is to do the inner work necessary to align or properly position our feeling, thought and actions in accord with Aware Presence and Unshakable Certainty—as shown in the graph below.

LVR TRUE ADDRESS INNERMOST IDENTITY	LVR WRONG ADDRESS SURFACE IDENTITY
Aware Presence that aligns with	Conditioned Self-Image and Briar Patches that align with
Clear and positive feelings that generate self-assurance and conviction that align with	Confused and negative feelings that generate fear and self-doubt that align with
Positive thoughts that support Certainty that align with	Negative thoughts that support Uncertainty that align with
Sure and confident action that aligns with	Unsure and hesitant action that align with
A creative, inspired, original and open life that is well-lived, loved and understood, that aligns with	An uncreative, uninspired, imitative and narrow life that is lived in ambivalence and confusion that aligns with
Happiness and fulfillment	Unhappiness and dissatisfaction

Let's turn now to the next chapter where we'll pull some things together before we move on to see the powerful impact that Unshakable Certainty can have on your work, your relationships and your health.

CHAPTER 6
Connecting The Dots

Before we move on to see the powerful difference Unshakable Certainty can make in your work, in your relationships and in your health, let's pause together briefly to do something important.

Rest here with me for awhile to consider a clear and straightforward way you can think about what Unshakable Certainty is and why it's so important for you to find it. We want to boil down all you've learned into a concise statement so you can have a clear picture of what you're after and why. You can keep this simple and concise statement in a corner of your mind as a reminder and as a link to a more in depth and thorough consideration of what it is, and what it can do for you.

<u>In a nutshell, Unshakable Certainty is an accurate, comfortable state of awareness that allows you to know what is real and right for you.</u>

When you expand on our nutshell statement, you can recall that Unshakable Certainty is a self-assured and secure state of mind that's rooted in who you deeply are. It's a sure, calm, aware state of mind that allows you to feel great about who you are and excited about your life again. When you find, cultivate and live from Unshakable Certainty you can feel relaxed and comfortable in your own skin—while you know you can handle pretty much any situation that comes your way.

THE UC PROCESS™ AND UNSHAKABLE CERTAINTY

A brief story can point to how the UC Process™ can align your feeling, thought and action with Unshakable Certainty by liberating you from a conditioned past that traps you in an identity too small for who you truly are.

The story is about an elephant named Little Guy. Little

Guy as a baby was tied to a small wooden post for long periods of time, a post he couldn't budge. Years later when he was huge and strong, Little Guy could have ripped this small post right out of the ground. But when tied to it, he just stayed put because his conditioned Self-Image made him feel that he was Little Guy, an elephant who wasn't strong enough to break free. After he did the UC Process™ for awhile, Little Guy changed his name to Big Guy and ripped that sucker right out of the ground, and now he goes wherever he wants to, whenever he wants to. Big Guy now roams around with benefit of an accurate, comfortable state of awareness that allows him to know what is real and right for him.

The Process is like a slide that you can ride into Aware Presence. Aware Presence is not awareness _of_ anything; it is a state of being fully awake here and now. The View from Aware Presence is the Free Position—one that allows you to let go, release and stand free from any flow of thought or feeling that could pull you too far into fear, worry, self-doubt and insecurity.

When you are in Aware Presence, uncertainty based thoughts and feelings come and go like reflections, reflections that don't disturb or distract you. If you do get distracted, then the Process will protect your mind from getting carried away and confused by its own contents—the trap door to shaky uncertainty—by refreshing your connection to Aware Presence.

Aware Presence and the Free Position are two sides of the same coin. When fear, self-doubt or worry is upon you, the Free Position allows you to host these states of mind from a relaxed awareness that is separate from these states of mind. This clear and relaxed awareness is completely open and free; it just sees what is. It has no agenda, and it doesn't grasp onto things or outcomes. It is beyond hope and fear; and it remains true to itself—no matter what happens.

Although Unshakable Certainty cannot shield you from life's unavoidable trials, from the heartaches, anguish and losses that will inevitably come your way, it will help you to face and endure their harsh sting with a strong, open heart. No matter what happens, as long as you are aware and connected to Unshakable Certainty, you can live your life with gusto as an adventure that you can define in your own terms.

DIRECT EXPERIENCE IS THE ACID TEST

To really understand how Aware Presence creates Unshakable Certainty you must experience it for yourself. The reason the Process is so powerful is that it allows you to find Unshakable Certainty, as an experience, when you need it. This 5-Step practice represents the cutting-edge art and science of finding, cultivating and living in the Now.

There's a lot of lively talk today about living in the Now and being present, but it's just talk unless it can be lived. There's no use talking about a treasure you can't find or praising a light you can't see. The Process can turn on your lamp of Aware Presence so that it illuminates Unshakable Certainty well enough for you to claim it.

The UC Process™ allows you to refresh your connection to Unshakable Certainty moment to moment. As a result, the Process makes it possible for you to find Unshakable Certainty, resolve all your doubts about what it is and develop your capacity to connect to it at will.

When you can do this, you'll be able to live from an accurate, comfortable state of awareness that allows you to know what is real and right for you. Then you'll have:

• more clarity about who you are;

- more self-assurance about your abilities;
- more conviction about what you want, need and love;
- more joy and peace; and
- more power to act decisively.

With Unshakable Certainty you'll be able to connect to who you deeply are and to the relaxation, awareness and creative energy that can allow you to create three things that especially make this life worth living:

1. Work that matters, that's fun and that fits who you deeply are.
2. Relationships that flourish in a steady supply of love and friendship.
3. Health, well-being and a long-lived life that's an adventure.

Let's now turn to explore how living from <u>an accurate, comfortable state of awareness that allows you to know what is real and right for you</u> can make your work life something truly special.

CHAPTER 7

Unshakable Certainty & Work

"I LIKE WHAT IS IN WORK, THE CHANCE
TO FIND YOURSELF."
—JOSEPH CONRAD

"LET THE BEAUTY WE LOVE BE WHAT WE DO."
—RUMI

"BLESSED IS HE WHO HAS FOUND HIS WORK.
LET HIM ASK NO OTHER BLESSEDNESS."
—THOMAS CARLYLE

"WORK IS ONLY WORK IF YOU'D RATHER
BE DOING SOMETHING ELSE."
—RAY PRINCE

In a nutshell, Unshakable Certainty is an accurate, comfortable state of awareness that allows you to know what is real and right for you. With this chapter, we begin to see just how much knowing what's real and right for you can mean to your life.

People who find and live from Unshakable Certainty love their work.

They have a solid connection to their Innermost Identity. They have discovered something very special—they've discovered a direction for their work that is right for them, a direction based on who they truly are.

If you can Relocate to your True Address and envision your work life from there, your unique needs, abilities and interests will come together in a sense of purpose that will lead you to work that fits who you really are. With Unshakable Certainty, you will have the self-assurance and conviction you need to grow your sense of purpose into a vision for your work life that brings you great joy and meaning.

In contrast, if you lack self-assurance and conviction, it's unlikely that you will find your work, because you'll live within the narrow confines of your conditioned Self-Image. Your work will focus on what you feel you should or must do, and on the kind of work valued and promoted by your family or by your social group or you'll simply take what work is "available."

Incidentally, success doesn't solve the problems this kind of work inevitably brings, because no matter how successful you are in terms of fame, power, position and income, if you're not doing what you want and love to do, your work will become a struggle, a struggle that will pull the quality of your life down. When your work is deeply sourced from your Innermost Identity, in contrast, it becomes joyful play and it elevates the quality of your life as a result. As Noel Coward noted, "Work is more fun than fun." A statement supported by Thomas Edison tells us how good it can be to work from a deep sense of purpose. In his words, "I never did a day's work in my life. It was all fun."

Without Unshakable Certainty, you will hesitate to cast a vision for your work like that of Coward's and Edison's because you won't expect or believe that you can realize it. And even if you could craft a vision based on a felt sense of purpose, shaky uncertainty will leave you ill-equipped for the ups and downs and confusing turns that everyone must face on the road to creating truly meaningful work.

The risk is that if you lack a dream or a vision or the security and self-confidence needed to do something special, you'll work for money, power, safety or to just put food on the table. You might decide to go into law, sales, construction or dentistry, but probably not because you really want to, but because you believe that these lines of work will pay well and allow you to fulfill your obligations, including your obligations to your family and cultural conditioning.

Work will then become something you feel obliged to do, not what you truly want to do. We're not making any value judgments here; it's not that one line of work is better than any other; it's whether or not we are doing work that truly fits with the needs, wants and interests of our Innermost Identity. Are we working out of a sense of deeply felt purpose is the question. When you have Unshakable Certainty, you do what you want and love to do and that's why your life is so joyful and fulfilling.

It's not necessarily the case that you need to choose or create one fixed and permanent line of work, but rather that you are truly alive doing what fits who you are. It's not uncommon for remarkable work lives to include many changes. Someone might succeed in business and then return to school to build a teaching career, only to go off after two years of teaching to create and start up a series of alternative schools. If we connect the dots on this kind of work life, we'll find a thread that runs through it, a thread of Unshakable Certainty that grants the clarity and power to act and create.

When you are in Aware Presence and the Free Position, you are open, free and aware now, and you are not tethered to a fixed and narrow sense of yourself based on past conditioning. Life energy can flow to you and through you, and like a jazz musician who improvises what she's playing in that very moment, your work and your life will become a creatively improvised affair. You won't need sheet music to figure out what to play. Aware Presence in action is the fuel and substance of adventure.

And when you work out of what you want and love to do,

you can feel free in your work, not burdened, which is a major triumph, one recognized by the famed British philosopher Robin Collingwood, who saw that, "Perfect freedom is reserved for those who live by their own work and in that work do what they want to do."

Working with deep purpose and with love reflects an ancient wisdom that too often seems lost today. Thousands of years ago the great Chinese teacher and Sage Confucius saw exactly what we're talking about. He put it this way: "Choose a job you love, and you will never have to work a day in your life."

HOW TO RETIRE EARLY

Choosing the work you love and working with deep purpose in freedom is the master key to transforming your work life. The goal is not to retire and stop working; it's to retire early from work that you don't want to do anymore so you can do the work you really want to do, work that makes you happy.

If you dislike your work, if it just doesn't ring your bell, the chances are good that you'll feel that something is missing in your life. When your work is deeply rooted in something that turns you on—in contrast—a special energy fills your life, an energy that just can't be there otherwise. There's a special energy that pours forth when you are aware and active doing what is inherently rewarding, a life energy that can deliver very high levels of work and life satisfaction.

This simple truth is often demonstrated by young children because they live in the moment and they only do what's real for them. My three-year-old nephew Jack is a good example. He loves trucks. Big ones, little ones, red, blue or yellow—no matter—he just loves them all. When he's playing with a truck he is in heaven. He pushes and pulls his truck with a passion, sometimes smiling, sometimes making "truck noises" and other times just looking at his truck in wonder. He especially loves orchestrating little games, games that only he understands that involve coordinating his trucks on some kind of mission.

Not long ago he got a truck big enough to sit on and ride; his joy and delight were beyond telling. And for Christmas his grandfather arranged for a visit from the town Santa Claus who came by his house on a fire truck. Jack went for a ride with Santa, but the truth was that Jack's awe, joy and wonder had little to do with Santa. The real prize for Jack was riding on the huge red fire truck. If you can work doing what you love to do from who you deeply are, with great self-assurance and conviction—that will be reward enough. Katherine Hepburn put it very well when she said, "As for me, prizes are nothing, my prize is work." She obviously found the master key for creating work that was part of her life adventure.

Many years ago psychologists thought that all human motivation was reducible to satisfying physical needs—for comfort, food, safety and so on. Then some fascinating studies showed that we have psychological needs that can be just as strong as our physical needs. The studies showed that we have a deep inner psychological need to be effective and competent, to use ourselves well, especially doing something we love to do. The satisfaction of these needs is an inner affair. It's independent of external reward.

The results showed that all human beings are inherently motivated by psychological needs to be effective and competent doing things that are personally meaningful. Creating work that meets these needs brings deep satisfaction and fulfillment and a good dose of the magic of some of what really makes life worth living.

I've worked with a lot of people at midlife, people who

have had to face a harsh fact: Their work has no connection to who they really are. They feel lost, angry and stressed out when they discover that they went into a line of work for all the wrong reasons, reasons that typically include the social and family pressures they faced about "making good money" or having "respect and status" or "keeping the family business going" or because they felt "unable or unqualified" to do what they wanted to do, and so on.

This discovery that our work is not based on our sense of purpose, on what we really love, want and need, can come as a shock once it really sinks in. It can leave us depressed and at risk for family problems and for stress-related illnesses.

This is no small matter, for if your work lacks meaning, something deep within you will suffer and in extreme instances, even die. As Dostoyevsky, the renowned Russian writer and keen observer of the human condition wisely noted, "Deprived of meaningful work, men and women lose their reason for existence." He was right— consider this: More people die of heart attacks on Monday morning between the hours of 8 and 9 a.m. than at any other time of day or day of the week. Why? Because they are going off to work they hate, work that has little or no importance or meaning for who they truly are. Why do they do this? Because they are plagued by uncertainty. They live from a conditioned Self-Image that breeds fear, confusion and self-doubt. Stuck in Views where they feel emotionally confused and unsure of themselves, they choose or create work that has no real bearing on who they are and what they truly want and love.

Fortunately, midlife is a time when our Innermost Identity makes a strong move to turn the second half of our lives in the direction of depth and meaning. Midlife chaos is often best read as a wake up call, a call to find and work from the deepest and most real parts of ourselves. The reason for this wake up call is clear: The second half of our life is no longer a dress rehearsal, it's the real thing. Time passes quickly and there's a lot at stake—and something in us knows that.

THE MUSTARD STORY

Let me tell you a story that puts the time issue into nice perspective. I call it the Mustard Story, one that pretty well explains what's at stake when we forget who we really are, and when we lose or can't find our sense of purpose.

The Mustard Story is all about our needing mustard, going to the grocery store to get it and then arriving home with two bags of groceries—but with no mustard. Because we got distracted, we actually forgot what we went to the store for, until we returned home.

Life lived from shaky uncertainty is like that. Imagine that we came to earth to have an adventure, but we got distracted by fear and self-doubt and we settled for something far less. <u>It's as if we forgot to do what we came here for.</u> Then time runs out and on our death beds, we slap ourselves in the forehead and say, "My God, I forgot the Mustard!" Working from your unique purpose and vision is a critically important part of "Remembering the Mustard."

Whether you remember the Mustard in your youth, at midlife or in older age is not important. What's important is that you remember it, and so what's important is that you build your work on Unshakable Certainty—so that you can remember it. If your work is sourced from a deep sense of purpose, if it's part of your life adventure, then it will bring fire, heat and light to your life, and it will make you feel good—more energized and more alive.

Let's now take a look at what this deep sense of purpose actually is.

FINDING THE WORK WE LOVE

To sum up briefly, if your work life is to have great meaning, your work must bear the stamp of your personal vision and your unique aims, interests and abilities. Because these things cannot be found from or in your conditioned Surface Identity, you must find ways to move beyond it and into who you more deeply are. To find your vision and purpose you need self-knowledge and awareness, and ultimately you need to free yourself from the conditioned Locations, Views and the Realities they define. Then you can find and operate from Aware Presence; you can be energized by the creative river that is always flowing to you in the Now. This river does not flow through your Wrong Address.

Because the Unshakable Certainty Process™ fosters deep self-knowledge and awareness, the self-knowledge and awareness you need to awaken and Relocate to your True Address, it can be a tremendous resource for you to discover how to create work that really connects to and expresses who you deeply are.

The Process can help you to discover and grow the unique "germ" of your purpose, the special seeds of your unique interests, talents and abilities that you were born with and that you can develop into work that is right for you. The great poet James Russell Lowell put it this way: "For every person born into this world their work is born with them." Lowell's sentiment was echoed by Susan Blow who noted: "To each man is reserved a work which he alone can do."

This is not to say that your life is predetermined or predestined in some way. It is to say that you're a unique being, with interests, talents and loves that are special to who you are. In my nephew Jack's terms, he might say, "I love working with trucks, what do you love to work with?"

Work does not have to be something we just do for money. The aim is to have your work life express who you truly are and be able to earn a living doing so. In fact, many successful money makers start out doing the work they love and the money just follows. David Shakarian, the founder of General Nutrition, makes the point this way. He tells us that: "I never worked a day in my life. It's not work when you love what you're doing."

The point is not that we can forget about paying the bills and feeding the kids if we just wish upon a star to do the work we love. The point is that when we connect to our Innermost Identity and our deep sense of purpose, we tap into a powerful source of energy to work hard to create something special in our work lives.

There's no phony magic here. The real magic is that if we find ourselves and believe in what we find, then hard work can make our work and financial dreams come true. It happens all the time.

Let's look more closely at how we get to do the work we love and to love the work we're doing. Keep in mind that the first and foremost thing we need to find is Unshakable Certainty.

REMEMBER—LOCATION, LOCATION AND LOCATION

Recall that the three most important things we need to know about finding Unshakable Certainty are Location, Location and Location. This is so important that it's worth repeating briefly so we can bear in mind why this is so.

- Your Location determines your View.
- Your View defines your Reality.
- Your Reality is what you experience as real.

Put simply, if you connect deeply with yourself and work from there, you'll find the magic of deep purpose that can make your work play. To do this you need to be in the right Location to know what you want to do. Your job, your work, your career is your "occupation" and your occupation, according to Webster's Dictionary, is "the principle business of one's life." That's really a bull's eye definition. Real work IS the main business of our life.

The core of the word "occupation" is occupy, and occupy means to dwell, live in, to reside or inhabit. The bottom line is that the Location of your identity is where you live, and where you live determines your vision of work. Unshakable Certainty will allow you to think big about your work, because it represents a Location that is beyond the fear and self-doubt that hold most people back from finding out what they want to do and then doing it.

The goal is <u>not</u> to find and Relocate to your deepest identity, Aware Presence, and then just sit there. Rather, it's to strengthen your connection to it so you can work with Unshakable Certainty. Your certain conviction becomes unshakable as your awareness and knowledge become steady and unwavering.

Summing up, let's take a look at a graphic display of the difference between working from Unshakable Certainty vs. working from shaky uncertainty.

Unshakable Certainty	Shaky Uncertainty
Work Based on Want and Love	Work Based on Should or Must
Work Rooted in Unique Germ and Purpose	Work Rooted in Conditioning and Confusion
Work as Adventure	Work as Obligation
Work that is Fulfilling	Work that is Boring
Work that Energizes You	Work that Exhausts You
Work Challenges are Creative Opportunities	Work Challenges are Overwhelming Problems
Work has Significant Meaning	Work has Little or No Meaning

WHAT A DIFFERENCE UNSHAKABLE CERTAINTY CAN MAKE: A CASE STUDY

In my work with many hundreds of clients, patients and students over the years, I've witnessed the remarkable difference that Unshakable Certainty can make in a person's work life. Again and again I've seen that when someone connects with who they really are, they can choose or create work that's really right for them. Their work makes them happy and turns them on because it fits who they truly are.

Two young men come to mind whose lives tell an interesting story about Unshakable Certainty. Rick and Bill were both clients of mine seven years ago when they were in their early thirties. They both came from similar backgrounds; both were good men with strong dreams for the future.

I talk with Rick and Bill regularly so I know their situation well, and I have their go-ahead to tell you something about their work lives. Both are married with children and they live and work in the same city and in the same business: Crossroads Counseling Center. But there's one big difference. Bill owns the business, while Rick works for him as a staff counselor.

Bill is crazy about his work—he's doing what he wants and loves to do. His work means a great deal to him. It's like a sand-box filled with toys that he can play in. Rick just works for a living; he's doing what he must do to pay his bills, plan for his kid's education and for his retirement. Rick's work doesn't mean a lot to him. He even finds it boring a lot of the time, and he just does it because he has to. Rick feels that as a child he had to go to school and now as an adult he has to go to work. The fun in his life begins only when work lets out.

Bill makes strong money, many times more than Rick does. The difference in their incomes shows in the homes they live in, the cars they drive, the clothes they wear, the vacations they take and the donations they make.

At the end of the day Bill looks and feels like the day just began, his supply of energy seems endless, and he almost feels sad that the day is ending. He loves working to solve the creative challenges involved in running a first-rate counseling center; he's constantly reading, attending seminars and hiring the best consultants so he can do the best job possible.

Rick on the other hand, looks and feels exhausted by early afternoon, and he needs a steady supply of coffee to keep him going. He almost feels sad that the work day ever got started, and he feels pretty low by nightfall on Sunday when his week-end is just about over. By the end of most work weeks, Rick feels burnt out and overwhelmed by client and administrative problems that feel unsolvable—they really weigh him down.

Now just what makes this huge difference in Bill and Rick's work life? It's that Bill is working from a clear sense of purpose based on who he deeply is—he loves his work; whereas Rick is just working. Rick just works out of a sense of uninspired obligation and he doesn't particularly care for what he's doing. The truth is that Bill is no more intelligent than Rick is. Actually, Rick did a lot better in school and in his first job. Rick actually seemed to have a lot more going for him; he was more personable and he came from a family more able to give him both emotional and financial support. Bill was, in fact, the less successful person up until that time, and at one point, he nearly got fired from a job because he was doing so poorly.

The circumstances behind Bill's poor job performance brought him to a crossroads; he faced a fork in the road, one where he had to make a choice. He could choose to fail or he could choose to take a good hard look at himself and to come to terms with what was going on.

Bill chose to take a look, and what he found was that not only had he no clear or stable sense of purpose or direction in his life, but he didn't like himself at all. And he felt bitter about a lot of things, especially about his relationship to his father, a father Bill could never seem to please. Bill was afraid not to do what was expected of him, and not only was he clueless about what direction to head out in on his own, but his self-doubt and insecurity made it impossible for him to even try.

In our work together, what Bill discovered was that he was glued to his Wrong Address, his conditioned Self-Image and he was vulnerable to frequent Briar Patch falls, sometimes many every day. Once he learned the Unshakable Certainty Process™, he took to it like a fish takes to water. He mapped his conditioning and his Briar Patches, and he began to recognize the sound of his own voice.

The more he used the Process, the more he developed the self-knowledge he needed to wake up and take control of his life. He developed the unshakable self-assurance and conviction that he could run his own business—he wanted to be his own boss. Bill wanted to stop trying to please his father, including the version of his father that lived in his own head, a version that was a huge Briar Patch. Bill wanted to be free to start pleasing himself instead. His needs, interests and abilities lined up around building a dynamic first-rate business that could really help people negotiate their own "crossroads" in life, whatever they might be. Bill's work vision was based on a clear sense of purpose, one that set his work life on fire with the energy and focus needed to create exactly what he wanted. Bill's motto became: "Whatever it takes."

The obvious good news is that Bill's crisis became both an opportunity for turning his life around and for defining the purpose and vision of what would become his business. He truly loves his work and it embodies who he is and what he values. Rick is a good guy with a great family, but, once again, he just works for a living.

We need Unshakable Certainty to make the most out of our work lives and to make our work life part of our life adventure. It also makes possible another very important part of that adventure—love and relationship.

Let's turn to them now and see why.

CHAPTER 8

Unshakable Certainty
Love & Relationship

"IN REAL LOVE YOU WANT THE OTHER PERSON'S GOOD.
IN ROMANTIC LOVE, YOU WANT THE
OTHER PERSON."
—MARGARET ANDERSON

"THIS IS THE MIRACLE THAT HAPPENS EVERY TIME
TO THOSE WHO REALLY LOVE; THE MORE THEY GIVE,
THE MORE THEY POSSESS."
—RILKE

"IT IS ONLY WHEN WE NO LONGER COMPULSIVELY NEED SOME-
ONE THAT WE CAN HAVE A REAL RELATIONSHIP WITH THEM."
—ANTHONY STORR

People with Unshakable Certainty have fantastic relation-ships.

They have what it takes to make deep and strong relation-ships, and they know that great relationships are made—they don't just happen. One reason they know this is that they've taken the time and acquired the know-how to make a strong relationship with themselves.

People with Unshakable Certainty know themselves well, they're connected to who they truly are, they've mapped their Briar Patches and they have access to the Free Position and to Aware Presence. This allows them to enjoy the ties, bonds and connections they have with people as the sweet spot of life's adventure. They treasure their relationships more than their possessions.

If you can Relocate to your True Address, you would be better able to give and receive love, caring and commitment to and from your spouse, partner, friends and family, than you could if you did your relating from your Surface Identity. If you look carefully, it's easy to understand why this is so. If you're stuck at the surface in your conditioned Self-Image, you won't be on solid ground, and you'll often be shaky and uneasy about who you are. It will be as if you don't really own yourself, and if you don't own yourself, then you can't really give who you are to others. If you're insecure and uncertain about yourself, you'll feel too afraid and ill-at-ease to get close and intimate with another person and so, like your relationship with yourself, your relationships with others will live at the surface.

When you find Unshakable Certainty and map your Briar Patches, you will be able to see and appreciate the other person for who they actually are, rather than confusing them as characters in your own Briar Patch-based movies. One reason that one out of two marriages tends to fail is the Briar Patch hell that can break loose between two people when they live together 24/7 under the same roof.

Note that for simplicity's sake, we'll make general reference to marriage in this chapter, but let's keep in mind that most of what we explore applies to all of our important long-term relationships, to all the bonds and attachments we're deeply committed to.

When you fall into a Briar Patch and become identified with its View, then you tend to see your companion or spouse in terms of that View. As a result, you'll experience them in terms of your Briar Patch Reality, and you won't have the slightest idea you're doing it. You'll feel convinced that your experience testifies to who they are rather than to your own Briar Patch View. Couples are at the mercy of what their partners don't know about themselves.

Couples very often star in one another's Briar Patch movies, and my experience working with hundreds of couples is that this is the rule, not the exception. No wonder so many marriages often end and end badly. And no wonder so many relationships that don't end—wind up looking more like temporary ceasefires rather than successful relationships. Moreover, if our family of origin movie is unfinished, it will show up in our marriage—no doubt. We need finish it on our own as does our partner.

Again, a good marriage is made, and you need more than a blood test and a marital license to make one. You need to be aware. And you need to be prepared to make marriage an adventure, and not a parking spot for your confused and uncertain life.

If your relationships are going to run deep, bring you happiness and be an adventure, you need to have a strong connection to who you are, one that gives you the self-assurance, security and awareness to give and receive love and friendship over the long haul. If you lack these things, then your relationships will be strained and filled with tension, problems and disappointment. We all hunger deep down for a successful loving connection to others, and many people suffer terribly because their relationships don't work well. And they suffer further because they really don't know why their relationships don't work. J. Paul Getty captured this sentiment well when he noted,

> "I hate to be a failure. I hate and regret the failure of my marriages. I would gladly give all my millions for just one lasting marital success."

Let's now consider some of the things that we need to see and understand to make sure that our relationships go well.

MAKING RELATIONSHIPS THAT WORK WELL

Although relationships are complicated, what makes them work well is simple: the capacity to give and receive love and friendship. And the friendship part is especially important for long-term committed relationships, including marriage. Feelings of passionate "romantic love" are not enough to make a relationship work, and they tend to fade anyway. As the famed philosopher Nietzsche commented,

> "The best friend is likely to acquire the best wife or husband, because a good marriage is based on the talent for friendship."

Two people who live at their Wrong Address and who are clueless about their Briar Patches will inevitably have trouble giving and receiving love and friendship. As a result, their relationships will become like a radio station that just won't tune properly, one filled with a lot of static and interference. All the static and interference results from two basic things that block love and friendship, the same two things that cause a lot of fear, self-doubt and uncertainty.

1. Identification with a conditioned Self-Image
When two people are unconsciously stuck in the narrow and fixed Views of their conditioned Self-Image, they have limited and inflexible maps for negotiating the territory of relationship. They'll see and experience each other from those fixed Views.

2. Unmapped and unresolved Briar Patches
When two people are cut off from the hurts and wounds from their past relationships, these hurts and wounds will without

doubt leak into their present relationship and cause confusion and damage. This goes on "under the radar"—it's unconscious and therefore especially dangerous.

When you look carefully at what a relationship demands and requires, this makes perfect sense. And it seems unreasonable that anyone would marry or have a long-term relationship without being certain that they had or could get what they need to make it work. No one would volunteer to drive to a place a hundred miles away without knowing they had or could find the gas they need to get there, and yet people volunteer to get married as if marriage had some automatic pilot switch that would take care of everything.

Let's look at this more closely, because it's what sets the stage for the problems in marriage and in all forms of romantic relationship—and our task is to learn how to avoid them.

THE VIEW OF RELATIONSHIP THROUGH ROSE-TINTED GLASSES

The trap door into the harsh times of relationships that don't work well begins with the fact that our society offers us an unrealistic View of relationship, and especially of marriage. It's a View of marriage and love seen through rose-tinted glasses, one that denies the facts. It's not real. It's probable that you downloaded some or all of this View and that you need to upgrade it.

What is real is that marriage is hard work, and until you connect with who you truly are, you can't muster up what a marriage needs to survive, let alone thrive and flourish.

I've worked with many pained and worn out couples who thought that the formula for a successful marriage was romantic love, good intentions, a nice wedding, a mortgage and a child or two. When I press them on what else they might need, the most common response is love; couples in trouble feel that the problem is that they've fallen out of love. They don't really understand what interferes with the flow of love and friendship within their relationship. If they could put their troubled relationship under a microscope—what they'd find is shaky uncertainty.

Most couples in troubled relationships have no idea that their good intentions count for very little, and that they need the knowledge and the tools to make a marriage work, grow and prosper. They've bought into the unrealistic images about relationship, unrealistic images that film, television and music feed to us every day.

Another rose-tinted idea that couples bring into their work is that God wants them to stay together and that God is especially interested in their marriage working out. I am in no position to confirm what God wants or not, but I think that God may be too busy to attend to what we need to take care of ourselves. God may not want us to get cavities or have our teeth fall out, but it's our job to brush them.

Many couples blame financial tension for their problems, and while financial tension can indeed create relationship tension, it's actually a small factor in relationships that don't work well. The only difference between couples who make $40 million a year and couples who make $40 thousand a year is the cost of the home and furniture they fight and suffer in and on. This is not just a funny comment, it's the truth. I have seen it again and again. I've watched couples hold hands and look dreamily at one another while making plans to build multi-million dollar homes only to be divorced within one or two years after moving into them. Money is not that big of a deal.

Individuals in relationships that don't work out well, regardless of income level, share some things in common. They are as follows:

- They View romantic relationship and marriage from rose-tinted glasses.
- They lack Unshakable Certainty in their own lives and they are looking for it in relationship.
- They have no idea that being locked into fixed Views and swimming in Briar Patch infested seas are what really cause their relationship problems.
- They don't grasp what really shuts down the flow of love and friendship within their marriage and so they don't know what to do about it.
- They suffer from a lot of emotional confusion and uncertainty over who or what is responsible for the relationship not going well.

In sharp contrast, people in relationships that work very well look much different. Let's turn to them now to explore just why this is so.

THE JOY OF RELATIONSHIPS THAT WORK VERY WELL

Relationships that work well are a delight. They work because the people in them have the skills and knowledge to make them work. They know how to support a relationship and how to grow it into a mutual adventure of love and friendship.

Because people in relationships that work well have found Unshakable Certainty within themselves, they don't make the error of looking for it in other people. They share the following additional characteristics in common:

- They have grown beyond the limits of their conditioned Self-Image.
- They are connected to who they truly are.
- They have mapped and worked on their Briar Patches.
- They can access the Free Position and Aware Presence.

These qualities can make a remarkable difference in your relationships. Here's why. What people in marriages that work well know, that people in troubled marriages don't know at all, is that the lessons for making a good marriage often come in the form of difficulties and challenges.

It takes a keen eye for you to recognize difficulties and challenges as lessons and not to mistake them as unsolvable problems or evidence that you or your partner are bad or wrong.

When the oil light goes on in your car, you know you need oil. You don't need to get rid of the car or drive it until it breaks down completely. You simply need to get oil. Difficulties in your marriage (and all relationships) light up the opportunities for you to see what your marriage needs. Challenges and difficulties are like fingers pointing at what you need to see about yourself, about your partner, or about what is going on between you.

Moreover, conflict, resentment, boredom and anger can be a natural part of your intimate relationships. They come with the normal territory of long-term intimacy, and you need to know how to View them properly if you are to deal with them effectively.

THE PROCESS AND MAKING RELATIONSHIPS THAT WORK VERY WELL

Great relationships require strong "Location" skills, because if you can't be aware of your Location, of where you are, then things cannot possibly go well. Let's look at why this is so.

Recall the two things that block the flow of love and friendship in a relationship. Because Location determines View, and View defines Reality, if you're Located in the conditioned views of your Self-Image, then it is certain that you will be seeing your spouse according to your conditioned and limited Views as well.

And although you and your partner may share love and friendship, if you both live at the Wrong Address, then the love and friendship you give and receive will be weakened and harmed by the fact that you both often star in each other's Briar Patch movies. When two people in relationship get lost in each other's worst movies, they can't make sense of what's going on unless they have the eyes to see and the awareness to understand.

The ways you see your spouse depend upon where you are within yourself and what the View is from there. The person you "see" is not always out there; that is, you create or imagine them through your View of who they are. The fact is that your eyes are sometimes more like movie projectors than windows.

If you have no Locations skills, if you have not mapped your Briar Patches, and if you have no access to the Free Position—then you'll mistake your partner for the View you have of them. You'll see your partner as a cause of what you're feeling, of the frustration and conflict that echoes problems you had long before you met them. That's why it sometimes might feel as if Warner Brothers Central Casting has handpicked your spouse or partner after thousands of auditions—he or she seems to know all the right buttons to push to hurt you and drive you a little crazy.

If you have good Location skills, on the other hand, then you'll be able to Locate yourself, Breathe Free and Relocate to the Free Position, a position that will allow you to be aware of and defuse your Briar Patch state of mind rather than projecting it onto your partner. The Unshakable Certainty Process™ can be a powerful antidote to what typically poisons your long-term relationships. The Process trains you to host troublesome states of mind with awareness and it greatly reduces the likelihood that you will project from them onto your partner—or, if you do, it minimizes the chances that you'll stay wrongly committed to your Briar Patch View of them for too long.

Consider this. Imagine that you have a rejection and anger Briar Patch that your spouse triggers big time when she or he pulls away from you. If you have no Location skills, then when this Briar Patch hits, you'll feel hurt and angry at a level 8 on a 10-point scale. Not knowing any better, you'll blame your spouse for causing your level 8 feelings, and you'll be sure to let them know how you feel. You'll feel bitter and resentful. And your spouse will also feel unfairly treated and so on. The fact is that the trials of your intimate relationships can trigger your unmapped Briar Patches in the same way that lightning starts fires in a bone-dry forest.

If you are clueless about your projection-making tendencies, your partner will be at their mercy, and you will be unaware that you are relating to your own mind, not to your partner. Both of your Briar Patch wounds will throw gasoline on the fire of the inevitable conflicts and challenges that relationship brings. If you and your partner lack Location skills, you'll tend to fight with each other in win/lose terms. You'll both struggle to be "right" while making the other "wrong." Such conflict can be just a struggle between you for the power to define reality rather than a real attempt to see and solve problems. This goes on all the time and it often causes relationships to go badly. It just burns them up over time.

Now imagine the same situation but with one big change: You can now use the Process to build and grow strong Location skills. You can now recognize and host your Briar Patches for what they are and feel and act with Aware Presence. You feel in control, your spouse doesn't feel wrongly accused, and it feels safe and clear enough for love and friendship to continue to flow. This is exactly what causes relationships to go well. Awareness feeds and honors relationships.

Problems are expected in successful relationships. Not only are they expected, but they're welcome. They are welcome as creative opportunities for generating more awareness, more understanding, more partnership and ultimately, more adventure.

The greatest joy and adventure in relationship comes when you and your partner find Unshakable Certainty. Then you both will have the self-knowledge and self-assurance to deeply share who you are, and each of you can then function as trustworthy mirrors for one another. When one of you is stuck in a painful Location and View, for example, the other can offer reflection that allows the person stuck to break free. You can work together as an aware and loving team rather than getting stuck in conflicting positions as angry adversaries.

When a couple does the Process regularly, something truly remarkable can happen. There is a fragrance in the air when one of them falls into a Briar Patch or into a narrow and inflexible conditioned View. When one of them picks up the scent, they signal the other and they can both move into the Free Position and Aware Presence.

At this level of awareness and Unshakable Certainty, relationships work very well indeed because couples experience and solve problems on a win/win basis. Instead of trying to prove themselves right and their partner wrong, their stance is to try to understand what's going on.

If you and your spouse have Aware Presence, then problems between you become the raw material for making your relationship even stronger. Your relationship can be one that works quite well, one that hosts its conflicts and problems as lessons that need to be learned, not as battles that need to be won or lost.

THE MORE UNSHAKABLE CERTAINTY, THE GREATER THE RELATIONSHIP

The deeper you can go within yourself, the better your self-knowledge and the more stable your Aware Presence, and so the greater the quality of love and friendship you can give and receive. There are different kinds and degrees of love and friendship. Some are better suited than others to stand the test of time and to become part of your long-term life adventure. Let's turn now and look at some of these differences so that we can appreciate the connection between Unshakable Certainty and the range of possibilities that relationship can bring to our lives.

PHYSICAL LOVE RELATIONSHIPS

Let's begin with the kind of love often portrayed in music and film—romantic physical love driven by sexual chemistry. Strong feelings of romantic love and physical passion that initially form the bond in many intimate relationships are very powerful, but they don't last. Relationships based exclusively on this kind of love may offer you cherished memories because they gave you a taste of something special, but on their own, they can't ever provide the basis for great relationship.

Sexual chemistry and attraction determine physical love, love that can be quite powerful, but biology can sometimes be the only thing that brings you and someone else together. When physical attraction is most alive, you and your lover can barely stop thinking of each other because of the strength of your longing. This form of love can be intoxicating. It gives rise to many exaggerated feelings, and you can imagine that your lover is heaven sent to remedy your shaky uncertainty. You can't stop thinking of them and they seem to have the power to make everything OK, and to satisfy some of your deepest yearnings.

Through the amazing power of this kind of romantic love, you can glimpse your True Address and even feel the energy and inspiration of Unshakable Certainty. But romantic love based on physical chemistry alone will never deliver it to you. In time, you can become so fixated on your lover that you feel that you cannot live without him or her, at least not without unbearable pain and suffering. Your lover seems wonderful, necessary and perfect.

Although physical and romantic love can be very powerful, it always fades with time and familiarity. This can lead to disappointment, confusion, frustration and a collapse of your feelings of self-assurance and security. Your heart aches when the "magic dies."

If your physical love has quickly led to marriage and children, you can be in for a fierce introduction to just how badly relationships can go. You may wake up one morning confused about who this other person is and where all this furniture and these bills came from.

Let's turn to yet another kind of love that can bring pleasures and problems of a different sort.

EMOTIONAL LOVE RELATIONSHIPS

Emotional love is another kind of powerful love. Emotional love may or may not have a strong sexual component, but its distinctive feature is possessiveness. Your love for the other gets tied into an experience of owning them. They become "yours." This form of love also has its power—especially during the phase when both you and your lover are agreeable to being possessed. The bottom line here is the feeling that if you own your lover or partner, and if they own you, then you'll be safe, self-assured and secure. This is an indirect attempt to find Unshakable Certainty.

But when you or they no longer feel willing to be "owned" as each others' "one true love," all hell can break loose. Jealousy, mistrust and paranoia can show up, all fueled by the cruel return of shaky uncertainty in all its fury. You can feel abandoned and robbed of something that felt so very sweet while you "owned" it.

When we feel abandoned, the drama that emerges is one of tragic betrayal. And if we or our partner have wounds from being left behind, rejected and abandoned by others, then things can get very nasty. We actually begin to feel let down and deceived, and we begin to hate the other more and more, as our hurt swells. Danger lurks where the forces of fear and betrayal get out of control, as physical violence sometimes sadly confirms.

Ultimately, emotional love can lead you to anger and then to cold indifference. Emotional lovers can just stop caring for each other in an experience of "why bother." In the beginning, you feel sure that everything in your life will be fine, that you could own Unshakable Certainty, if only you could own the person you want, if only you could get them into your territory. At the end, the reverse is true. You wind up feeling that you have to get them out of your territory if you are to be free.

Only conscious love in some measure can connect you deeply to relationship with another person and to the adventure that relationship can bring—at its best. Let's turn to it now to see why this is so.

CONSCIOUS LOVE RELATIONSHIPS

The deepest form of love is conscious love. It's the basis of real relationship, but sadly it's not too common. As the insightful commentator on love, A.R. Orage, noted—"Conscious love rarely obtains between humans...." That's because conscious love only comes once we have found Unshakable Certainty. When we find Unshakable Certainty, we're no longer looking to our partner to relieve our fear, self-doubt and insecurity. We've taken care of that on our own because we're connected to who we truly are. Conscious love is awake and unselfish; it's the basis of relationship focused on the other.

Conscious love involves your selfless desire to have the person you love attain her or his greatest possibilities. That is, you want them to become everything that they can possibly be.

It's not that conscious love is present all the time, but rather, it's the wash on the canvas in your relationship. It provides the background and backdrop for the essential elements in the connection between you and your partner or spouse.

Unselfish love tends to stimulate the same in your partner for you. This kind of love involves a recognition and genuine appreciation and regard for who your partner actually is. With conscious love you enter into a real partnership with your spouse. A marriage based on conscious love requires you to put the needs of the relationship before your individual needs. You might say that you and your lover or spouse must pay the relationship before you pay yourself.

Conscious love is based on the realization that you can't really learn how to live with another person until you have some handle on being able to live with yourself. Until you move beyond your conditioned Self-Image and Briar Patch wounds, you cannot easily appreciate your partner for who they deeply are—rather than for what they can do for you.

Sometimes conscious love can rise from the ashes of burnt out physical or emotional love. Often this happens after periods of deep conflict and difficulty—if we have the resources to make our way out of them with love and understanding.

Summing up, let's take a look at a graphic display of a comparison between relationships with and without Unshakable Certainty.

Unshakable Certainty	Shaky Uncertainty
Conscious Love Present Focus on Spouse or Partner	Conscious Love Absent Focus on Self
Love and Friendship Flowing	Love and Friendship Blocked
Deep and Open Meaningful Conversation	Briar Patch Ceasefires with Guarded Conversation
No One is at Fault No One is Bad or Wrong	He or She is at Fault and Bad or Wrong or I am at Fault because I am Bad or Wrong
Conflict is Win/Win	Conflict is Win/Lose
Relationship Challenges are Creative Opportunities	Relationship Challenges are Overwhelming Problems
Relationship an Exciting Adventure	Relationship an Obligation and Safety Net

A CLOSE LOOK AT THE DIFFERENCE UNSHAKABLE CERTAINTY CAN MAKE: A CASE STUDY

Over the years, I've witnessed the incredible difference Unshakable Certainty can make in people's relationships. When two people connect with who they really are, then they can relate more deeply and more consciously. Their relationships become more open and more alive and more healthy and happy.

What excites me most is the power of the Unshakable Certainty Process™ to give couples the eyes, tools and certainty they need to see and do what's necessary to make their relationship grow and prosper. The Process is a remarkable practice for any committed relationship, because it's a practice that can keep open and even reopen a strong flow of love and friendship between two people.

Two couples come to mind who give us a chance to take a close look at the difference that Unshakable Certainty can make in a relationship. Jill and Tom Smith and Helen and John Plant each had two children, and they were similar in many other ways; the Smiths and the Plants were around the same age, they lived in neighboring towns, earned similar incomes and were members of the same faith. They came to me by way of their pastor, a man who knew of my use of the Process in my work with couples and groups of couples.

Jill and Tom Smith were married for eight years, Helen and John Plant for six. Both couples were thrilled about getting married; they felt sure they'd stay together forever. Their early romantic relationships were very passionate and filled with sexual excitement and the conviction that they were meant for each other. During the initial stages of their romance, Jill and Tom felt the same way that Helen and John did; both couples felt as if they "belonged together" and that as long as they had one another, then everything would be fine.

Obviously, both couples were very much alike. But there's one big difference. The Smiths are happily married today and their relationship is indeed an exciting adventure. The Plants were bitterly divorced a few years back, and they barely speak to each other today.

The difference between these couples is dramatic, but the cause for the difference is simple: Today there is a steady flow of love and friendship between the Smiths, whereas, for the Plants the flow shut down completely years ago.

The flow of love and friendship shut down and stopped for the Plants for the usual reasons it stops for most couples. It stops when each partner operates in relationship from the fixed and narrow Views of their conditioned Self-Image and when they have no awareness or knowledge of their Briar Patches.

Both of these couples really wanted to stay together when I first met them. The difference was that the Smiths were able to hang in there and get what they needed to heal their relationship and grow it into something special. The Smiths were able to learn the Process, and it gave them the knowledge they needed along with the tools to have what they wanted, which was to keep their love and friendship alive.

The Plants began to learn the Process, but they couldn't put it to use to get what they needed so badly. And without knowledge they just couldn't keep the relationship from shutting down. John Plant couldn't turn the corner and face that he needed to see and own things about himself; his View was that all he needed to see was Helen.

He saw some of his wife Helen's contributions to their difficulties, her anger and impatience, for example, but he was blind to how controlling and inconsiderate he was. And he failed to see that one reason Helen was prone to losing it with anger was that she felt helpless in the face of his insistence that he knew what was wrong between them. She was understandably enraged that, according to his fixed View, what was wrong in their relationship was always Helen. John felt this way, he really believed it and he was clueless that he was stuck in a Location with a View of Helen that didn't match up with who she really was. And that she was suffering as a result.

In truth John was throwing the same bricks at Helen that his father threw at his mother and at him. Like his father, John had to be right all the time or else. All conflict between John and Helen was win/lose, and John always had to win. Routine difficulties, such as agreeing on a time the kids should go to bed, became overwhelming problems, and real problems became near catastrophes. There was no meaningful conversation between them, and there were regular breaches in their fragile ceasefires. Being around them sometimes was like walking across a minefield—one never knew when things would just blow up.

The idea that John had an unknown Briar Patch wound around "power and control" was unacceptable to him. And getting him to see that his wound was caused by being on the other end of his father doing to him exactly what he was doing to Helen was like asking him to have a sex change operation without anesthesia.

The sad fact was that John's Safeguard was so fiercely protecting him from his Briar Patch wounds that he had a blind spot the size of California. He just couldn't see that he was destroying his relationship with Helen. He couldn't see that he was shutting down the flow of love and friendship. Because of his conditioned limitations, John could not experience the conscious love for Helen that would have allowed him to really see what life was like for her in their marriage. If he did, then he could have rescued them both from his inflexible Views and Briar Patch wounds.

An even sadder fact is that John became like his dad, because we often desperately protect ourselves by becoming like the people who harm, control and dominate us, a fact known in the lingo of psychology as "identifying with the aggressor." That's why so many kidnap victims and hostages can begin to resemble their captors. This "being like his father", of course, became another part of John's Wrong Address.

John's mother accepted John's father playing the role of Yoda, the Man Who Knew Everything, and John unconsciously wanted Helen to do the same. Helen refused to do that, and although she wanted her marriage to work, she just couldn't take it, so she filed for divorce. Helen wanted badly for her relationship to be an adventure, and unlike John's mother, she couldn't live with her marriage just being an obligation and a safety net.

In contrast to the Plants, Jill and Tom Smith saw the power of the Process right away and they were able to make use of it. Like the Plants, their marriage was stuck and troubled, the flow of love and friendship down to just a trickle. Their relationship over the years had become hard work, and they wondered where the excitement went and why it left.

When introduced to the idea that good marriages are hard work and had to be made, they both nodded so much it seemed like their heads would fall off. They liked the idea because it fit what they were going through and it gave them hope. At first, they devoted themselves to practicing the Process like two people who were thrilled about learning how to play tennis. They compared experiences and worked together to better understand and practice the 5 Steps. Their dedication to doing the practice and applying what they learned really paid off.

It helped them tremendously, because as the great soccer player Pele said, "Practice is everything." If you practice the Process, then everything falls into place as you learn what it's about. It all happens naturally because the Process is rooted in your capacity for being aware and awake. It enhances a capacity already in you; it doesn't add something that's foreign to what you are. What the renowned musician Bach said about playing music is also true about staying awake, about Aware Presence. As Bach put it, "There's nothing remarkable about it. All one has to do is hit the right keys at the right time and the instrument plays itself."

Jill and Tom just loved what they were experiencing as they practiced. When in conflict, they'd pause and do the Steps. Then they'd ask, "Where am I now?," and the question alone would lighten things up tremendously. Usually they'd get stuck arguing win/lose, but with the Process, the atmosphere changed and they began to think and feel win/win. They'd Locate themselves, Breathe Free and Relocate to the calm, clear state and later to the Free Position and to Aware Presence.

As Jill and Tom discovered their conditioned Views and as they mapped their Briar Patches, they began to share their discoveries. In their sharing, they began to share deeper versions of their inner "stories" together, and in the process more of their True Identity became known to themselves and to each another.

When you and your spouse or lover share your innermost identities, you are in essence exchanging the gift of gifts, an exchange that opens up your relationship to the territory of conscious love. And the territory of conscious love, once open, insures that the love and friendship between you will continue to flow—from the heart.

The Process began to enter into their daily lives; often they'd check in and ask each other: "Where are you now?" They became attuned to one another so that Tom could tell if Jill was feeling bummed out and vice versa, and they got good at helping each other recognize and break free from Briar Patch Locations. They also marveled over how free the Free Position actually was. Their typical conflicts, the ones that caused so many problems when fought win/lose, the ones over money, sex and the kids, were now conflicts that played out on a higher win/win level—because they could stand free and let go of the fear and self-doubt that lurks behind the need to win or to be right. Their problems became creative challenges that they now faced as a team playing on the same side.

Tom and Jill's connection to each other improved dramatically as they deepened their relationship and gained more and more self-knowledge. They woke up to the fact that the Unshakable Certainty they were looking for from each other was something they could get only from themselves. They were blown away by how deeply they could connect to their True Address while resting in the silence and stillness of Aware Presence, and their relationship has indeed become an adventure because it's now based on that connection.

Unshakable Certainty can help you make the most of your relationships. It can also make it possible for you to enjoy excellent health and exceptional levels of well-being.

Let's turn now to the next chapter to see how and why.

CHAPTER 9

Unshakable Certainty &
Health and Well-Being

"HEALTH IS THE GREATEST GIFT."

—BUDDHA

"PROLONGED STRESS CAN BADLY UPSET THE BIOCHEMICAL BALANCES IN YOUR BODY. THAT CAN IMPAIR YOUR IMMUNE SYSTEM AND LEAVE YOU OPEN TO INVASIONS OF CANCER CELLS AND DANGEROUS INFECTIONS. "

—DR. BRUCE MCEWEN

"....PEOPLE ARE DISTURBED NOT BY THINGS, BUT BY THEIR PERCEPTION OF THINGS...."

—EPICTETUS

"...IN OUR MODERN SOCIETY, STRESS DOESN'T ALWAYS LET UP. MANY OF US NOW HARBOR ANXIETY AND WORRY ABOUT DAILY EVENTS AND RELATIONSHIPS. STRESS HORMONES CONTINUE TO WASH THROUGH THE SYSTEM IN HIGH LEVELS, NEVER LEAVING.... "

—DRS. CHROUSOS AND GOLD

People with Unshakable Certainty typically enjoy excellent health and well-being. They feel better, look better and live longer than people who are weighed down by chronic uncertainty.

If you find and live from Unshakable Certainty, you'll have a good supply of high quality energy because your life will be lived beyond the energy draining fixed Views of your conditioned Self-Image and your Briar Patch wounds. You'll be connected to your Innermost Identity, a connection that will allow you to feel secure, self-assured and in control. As a consequence, you'll enjoy a positive outlook. You'll feel happy, upbeat, optimistic and excited about your life and about your possibilities, feelings that we now know to be strongly linked to health and well-being.

In sharp contrast, if you live from shaky uncertainty, your energy supplies will be chronically low because your energy will be depleted by stressful Waking Dreams triggered by your conditioned Self-Image and Briar Patch Views. If you are not connected to your Innermost Identity, you'll tend to feel unsure, afraid, in doubt and out of control. As a consequence, your outlook will be negative. You will feel unhappy, depressed and bummed out a lot of the time. And you will feel frustrated with your life and pessimistic about your possibilities, feelings that we now know to be powerfully connected to poor health and illness.

With Unshakable Certainty, you'll have something going for you that protects your health and well-being under all conditions. Because you are connected to the Free Position and to Aware Presence, you can short-circuit stress at its source, an ability that will protect you from chronic illness, premature death and the ravages of older age. This ability comes with Unshakable Certainty. Because you can short-circuit stress at its source you can do two things that people stuck at their Wrong Address can't do. You can:

- Prevent the chronic release of toxic stress hormones such as cortisol and epinephrine into your bloodstream.

- Flush out stress hormones from your bloodstream and tissues—as soon and as thoroughly as possible.

These two things are critical and necessary for preserving your health.

Stress hormones cause illnesses that kill more people each

year than do the causes of all other deaths combined. Recall that stress is a biochemical event. It's not just feelings of tension and strain; stress involves the release of toxic hormones into the body, hormones that can destroy your health.

The World Health Organization has identified stress as the number one health problem in the modern world. Dr. Paul Rosch, President of the American Institute of Stress, tells us why:

> "Stress is … a heavy contributor to heart disease, cancer, respiratory distress, lupus and many other life threatening illnesses."

Without Unshakable Certainty, your stress levels are more likely to be high. The higher your stress levels, the more likely you'll be plagued by an assortment of other lower tier stress driven health problems, problems such as anxiety, depression and the syndrome of "just not feeling well," along with nutrition and weight problems.

If you are troubled by shaky uncertainty, you'll be more inclined to self-medicate your distress with food and other mood-altering substances including drugs, alcohol and tobacco. You'll tend to medicate yourself to get relief from your stressful Waking Dreams and the Views that trigger them. When you feel shaky and uncertain, a drink or a smoke or a big chocolate brownie or a doughnut, can offer you short-term relief, but at a steep price you'll have to pay in the longer term.

And your fear, self-doubt and anxiety might lead you to join the ranks of those who seek relief from shaky uncertainty through prescription medications. More than 200 million people also take prescribed medications to manage symptoms caused by stress hormones. Medications of any kind are not always good solutions, however. They deal with the symptoms, but they don't deal with what causes the symptoms—the unnecessary release of toxic stress hormones caused by shaky uncertainty.

The bottom line is that your health is most determined by what you think and feel most of the time. And what you think and feel entirely depends on where you are within yourself. The fact is that if you put stress and all the illnesses and problems that stress causes under a high-powered microscope, what you'll see is shaky uncertainty along with everything that causes and accompanies it. Shaky uncertainty is the major cause of chronic stress, and so it's among the greatest threats to your health and well-being.

Let's turn now to understand just why this is the case.

HOW SHAKY UNCERTAINTY ERODES HEALTH AND WELL-BEING

The fact is that people who live at their Wrong Address are often troubled by fear, doubt and insecurity, and so they are at increased risk for health problems because they frequently fall into stress hormone-producing Waking Dreams.

If you lack Aware Presence, your Waking Dreams will of course be sourced by your inflexible Surface Identity and Briar Patch Views that can overtake you around any corner. Instead of realizing that your negative states of mind result from these Views, you'll wrongly believe that your feelings testify to literal and factual Reality, to something actually going on in your life in present time.

You won't understand the simple and powerful three-part knowledge base that is the rock solid foundation for Unshakable Certainty and for health as well. You'll recall that:

1. Your Location Determines your View.
2. Your View defines your Reality.
3. Your Reality is what you experience as real.

For this knowledge base to protect your health, you must own it experientially, as it can't just be three ideas you understand conceptually. You may understand a dance with your mind, but if you don't learn the dance through experience, then when the stage curtain goes up, you'll just stand there because you won't know what to do.

If you understand this knowledge base through felt and lived experience, then you will have found Unshakable Certainty. If you don't feel and live it, then it will just stay in your head as an interesting idea. Without experiential knowledge, you'll be more prone to states of mind that trigger stress hormones; states of mind such as fear, self-doubt, worry and anxiety—the Waking Dream monsters who roam the land of uncertainty. As a consequence, you will be set up for the number one cause of serious health problems, as follows:

- The predisposition to <u>View</u> and experience life and life events as stressful.

This predisposition will put you at great risk. It's what will leave your blood and tissues saturated in dangerous hormones such as cortisol and epinephrine. If you experience a lot of uncertainty, it's as if you live under chronic showers of acid rain, showers that erode your hope and wear your body out. Feeling anxious, insecure, inadequate and frustrated, you'll be driven into a never-ending array of uncertainty-based concerns and worries, worries that signal your inner pharmacy to release powerful hormones when they are not needed.

These hormones were designed and meant to protect you against the uncertainty of actual life-threatening physical danger, short-term danger that would require you to fight or flee for survival. They were not designed to protect you against the uncertainty monsters that populate your long-term Waking Dreams.

Any life situations that we find ourselves in can trigger these dreams and the stress-provoking monsters that inhabit them. To illustrate simply but clearly, let's imagine the following situation. A man named Frank is in the market for a new car. He is plagued by shaky uncertainty, and he has to choose between buying one of two cars, a Toyota and a Subaru. Just having to make the decision leaves Frank stressed out. All of a sudden he notices that he feels fear and worry, and it's clear that some rumbling is going on outside of his awareness. All Frank is aware of is that he's now very afraid that he might make the wrong choice; it's as if a voice keeps whispering in his ear, "Don't buy the wrong car—or else."

A few days after he buys the Toyota, Frank goes to the dentist. While in the waiting room he reads an article that praises the Subaru, the car he didn't buy. In the midst of having his teeth cleaned he suddenly falls into a lot of "buyer's remorse;" Frank becomes absolutely convinced that he blew it, that he bought the wrong car. Uncertainty takes him over and he feels just terrible. The Locations that generate this Waking Dream View include an inflexible Self-Image that operates with a stress hormone-provoking "perfection" download that goes like this:

- Capable and effective people make perfect decisions.
- I made a bad decision.
- Therefore I am an incapable and ineffective person.

As if this was not bad enough for Frank, his Briar Patch wounds now begin to kick in further. He unconsciously falls into a particularly thorny one loaded with shame and embarrassment, one connected to the many times his father scolded him for not doing things well enough, especially for not doing things as well as his younger brother Charles. Having no awareness of this Briar Patch, Frank experiences the flow of shameful feelings that leak from it—as feelings going on in the present, as feelings connected to the car purchase.

And so Frank leaves the dentist on the edge of falling deeply into a self-abusive Waking Dream fueled by his conditioned Self-Image and Briar Patches. While at a red light, what might you imagine pulls up beside him? The Subaru he didn't buy, the one he feels would have been the "right" decision. Frank looks at it and "sees" the car he should have bought. Like a fierce rip tide that pulls a swimmer out to sea, Frank is pulled into nightmarish Views and experiences of Reality that generate a ton of stress hormones. He feels like an idiot, an idiot who bought the wrong car.

Hours later Frank is still out to sea feeling like he's a bad and ineffective person who just can't do things right. He feels like he's just not good enough. Three beers, two slices of extra cheese pizza and a large bowl of nuts along with six cigarettes later—Frank begins to swim back to shore at 5 pm. Little does he know that that he's been in a five-hour Waking Dream. None of what stung and tormented Frank was true or real, but it sure seemed that way to him.

As simple and as amusing as this illustration is, it's not far from the truth of what happens to most people every day. You often View everyday life events as stressful, because life events often challenge your fixed Views and they trigger your Briar Patch issues.

Without Unshakable Certainty, you're always vulnerable to the sudden shifts in your states of mind, shifts that can trigger a stressful Waking Dream at any moment. If you have no connection to your deeper identity and Aware Presence, you'll lack the self-assurance, security and conviction that can only come when you have the ability to stay awake and host troublesome states of mind—instead of identifying with them.

Some people get knocked down and wiped out by shaky uncertainty, and as a result they lose their health and well-being. They lose any sense that life has some purpose or any basis for well-being and happiness. Hans Selye, the world renowned stress research pioneer explained years ago just how dangerous this can be when he noted that:

> "Mental tensions, frustrations, insecurity, aimlessness are among the most damaging stressors, ... studies have shown how often they cause migraine headache, peptic ulcers, heart attacks, hypertension, mental disease, suicide, or just hopeless unhappiness."

Stress hormones do an excellent job when you need them to prepare you for fight or flight to survive, but if released when you don't really need them, they can ruin your health. Moreover, these hormones leave you hyper vigilant to threat of any kind and so prone to more Views that trigger even more hormones.

A vicious cycle of shaky uncertainty and stress hormones and more shaky uncertainty and more stress hormones can take hold and even become a way of life—at the steep price of pain, illness and sometimes death. As Drs. Lyle Miller and Alma Dell Smith, two highly respected stress researchers, have explained:

> "Chronic stress destroys bodies, minds and lives. It wreaks havoc through long-term attrition. It's the stress

that the never-ending 'troubles' have brought....The *worst* (italics theirs) aspect of chronic stress is that people get used to it. They forget it's there. People ...ignore chronic stress because it is old, familiar, and sometimes, almost comfortable. Chronic stress kills .... People wear down ... physical and mental resources are depleted through long-term attrition...."

It's now clear why people who live at the Wrong Address and who are plagued by shaky uncertainty have more frequent and more serious health problems than do people who have found Unshakable Certainty.

Let's now turn to take a closer look at just how Unshakable Certainty enhances health and well-being.

HOW UNSHAKABLE CERTAINTY ENHANCES HEALTH AND WELL-BEING

To understand how and why Unshakable Certainty will enhance your health and well-being, let's note the powerful changes that will occur in your life if you find it. They are as follows:

1. You'll live beyond the limited Views of your conditioned Self-Image.
2. Your self-knowledge will become steady and reliable (as Steadfast Knowledge).
3. You'll re-educate Safeguard and Map your Briar Patches.
4. You'll Relocate to your True Address, to your Innermost Identity.
5. You'll be able to access the Free Position and Locate yourself in Aware Presence.

If stress hormones were an infection, then these five things would powerfully and permanently inoculate you against that infection. Accidents and genetically based health problems aside, these five characteristics ensure that if you find Unshakable Certainty, you will live long and well. Let's see exactly why this is so.

Recall that your conditioned Self-Image is your Wrong Address. It's a surface Location that predisposes you to a lot of stress because it binds you to shaky and inflexible Views. Being stuck in these Locations is like being confined to prison—you can't easily escape stressful experiences of Reality. Bear in mind that you think, feel and act in accord with your conditioned Self-Image—whether or not it's accurate. Think of Frank, the car buyer.

People with Unshakable Certainty are free from the stress that comes with living at their Wrong Address. They're no longer confined by wrong assumptions about who they are and so they're no longer trapped in stressful emotional confusion and Waking Dreams of fear, self-doubt, and insecurity.

If you Map your Briar Patches, you can then move around in life without being ambushed, dragged down and stressed out by falls into your Briar Patch Views. Think of Frank the car buyer again to see how easily such ambushes can happen. Your self-knowledge will be steady, you'll know yourself well, and so your Steadfast Knowledge will be able to bring Safeguard into present time.

This accomplishment frees you from having to fight stress-producing wars that ended years ago. Instead, you will be able to reeducate Safeguard to better focus on the interests sustaining the Aware Presence that's so vital to your happiness and well-being in present and future time. You'll be more happy, joyful and healthy because you will be able to let go and live beyond the obstacles that stand in the way of your happiness, joy and health.

If you can access the Free Position, you can host negative states of mind without being swept out to sea by them. You can be with fear for example, without being defined or possessed by it. You can let negative states of mind come and go, like passing clouds, without becoming stressed out by them. Your Aware Presence is like a bonfire that lights up the here and now well enough to keep you from being driven into excessive worry and concern about the past or future. This preserves your health and well-being as much as anything else. As the Buddha put it so well:

> "The secret of health for both mind and body is not to mourn for the past, not to worry about the future, or not to anticipate troubles, but to live in the present moment wisely and earnestly."

Incidentally, the benefits of Aware Presence are not limited to short-circuiting the release of stress hormones. The serene silence and stillness that you can find in Aware Presence triggers your body's powerful healing and recuperative powers. Aware Presence gives you access to mindbody experiences that bathe every cell in your body in health-giving energy. Deep relaxation, peace and serenity that are tonic for the body as well as for the soul come with the territory of Unshakable Certainty.

Let's revisit Frank the car buyer and re-imagine his car purchase as if he was a man who had Unshakable Certainty. While considering his decision to buy the Toyota or the Subaru, Frank hears that same voice in his ear: "Don't make a wrong decision," it says. But this time Frank lives beyond the confines of his conditioned Self-Image and he's mapped and worked his

Briar Patches, so that the painful experiences with his father are well known to him. The wounds are healed.

Frank recognizes the voice in his ear for what it is. He Breathes Free of it and Relocates to Aware Presence. He doesn't fall into a stress-provoking Waking Dream—he remains wide awake. He researches the purchase and he chooses the Toyota because it has good ratings and he likes its looks. Period.

Later on Frank reads the article praising the Subaru while sitting in his dentist's waiting room. He feels a twinge or two, but he Breathes Free and reconnects with the bottom line: he really likes the Toyota. Frank likes the way it drives and looks, and he's fully aware this decision was about buying a car, not about proving himself to his father or to anyone else. Frank was just having his teeth cleaned while he was having his teeth cleaned. That is, he was aware and present, he wasn't sitting there with his mouth open while off in some self-abusing, stress hormone-producing Waking Dream.

So after his visit to the dentist, Frank's at the red light on a Saturday afternoon, and alongside him pulls up the Subaru he chose not to buy. It looks good in the midday sun, and he even feels another little twinge of buyer's remorse that grabs at him, but he doesn't fight with the feeling—he just allows it and lets it go. Frank remains self-assured and connected to Aware Presence. The light changes to green and Frank drives away in a clear state of mind that has no doubt or regret about anything—let alone a Subaru.

In this rendition of the story, Frank demonstrates how Unshakable Certainty can enhance health and well-being by dramatically reducing the states of mind and Views that trigger the chronic release of toxic stress hormones.

This story also shows us another angle on how Unshakable Certainty increases our chances of living long and well. If you find and live from it, you'll have a better sense of perspective and proportion; you will be focused on the things that really matter in life, and you'll live life as an adventure, not as a confusing ordeal. You'll stay awake to the fact that you're here to Remember the Mustard, not to fret and worry on and on about concerns that can steal your time, stress you out and make you sick.

To better appreciate how much time and trouble shaky uncertainty can cost, let's now take a look at two health problems that have reached epidemic levels today: depression and obesity.

SHAKY UNCERTAINTY—THE ROOT OF DEPRESSION AND WEIGHT PROBLEMS

In many years of working as a clinical psychologist and as a medical psychotherapist, I've discovered that if we look closely at depression and weight problems under a microscope, we'll discover that they both rest on a foundation of stress-provoking shaky uncertainty. The problems are different but they're related. Not everyone who is depressed has difficulties with weight, although many do, but nearly every overweight patient I have ever seen has been depressed at some level.

Of course, there are forms of depression and weight problems that have a genetic and a biological basis, but they are in the minority. Medications for these problems can be a godsend. I am not against the use of medications altogether, as I sometimes use them short term for people undergoing difficult life transitions, such as the death of someone near and dear.

But I am against the unnecessary, costly and dangerous use of prescription drugs for problems that have no biological basis. A lot of the depression, sadness, frustration, anger and confusion that most people feel are feelings rooted in shaky uncertainty. The wear and tear of fear, self-doubt, anxiety, frustration and worry can be immense. The problem is not biological; the problem is the states of mind that rob people of hope, and without hope they feel at the mercy of forces beyond their control, a situation that IS depressing.

Physicians too often misdiagnose depression and obesity as biological illnesses because they look at these problems through "biological illness glasses," not through a clean microscope. Physicians do this for other reasons as well. Although a thorough examination of these issues is not the focus of this book, let's make brief note of these reasons for the sake of our discussion.

One is that our health care system is really a disease care system; it acknowledges health problems and "treats" them only after they occur. It does a terrible job understanding and preventing illnesses, especially those that have no biological basis, and most especially those caused by shaky uncertainty. The majority of medical physicians know very little about stress-related illnesses other than to medicate them after they occur (incidentally, physicians are now a high stress group with the highest suicide rate). People tend to do whatever their physician tells them to do, especially when it comes to taking drugs. But this can be dangerous to your health because physician errors are a leading cause of health problems and deaths in the United States.

This note raises another even more troublesome issue that underscores why depression and weight problems are so often misunderstood and misdiagnosed: The drug companies and the medical profession have formed an unholy alliance. Pharmaceutical companies now have too much control over the medical profession; they fund most medical research and they sponsor seminars, workshops and continuing education programs. Drug companies are spending about $15 billion a year on physician marketing. There is so much money to be made that professional ethics often get tossed out the window. As *New York Times* reporter Melody Peterson described in one of her stories:

> "Newly unsealed court documents reveal that physicians, in exchange for money, have allowed pharmaceutical sales representatives into their examining rooms to meet with patients, review medical charts and recommend what medicines to prescribe."

The temptations are great for there's huge money to be made by defining problems as illnesses and then selling drugs to relieve or to cure them. The drug industry is huge and powerful, more powerful than most people imagine, and it will do whatever it can to mold public opinion to support astronomical drug company profits. It markets to the fact that people want quick fixes for their problems whenever they can get them.

Consider the deceptive drug advertisements that now flood the media. By defining life problems as biological illnesses, consumers are persuaded that they need medication; they run to their physician's office looking for the relief promised by false advertising. And they fork over huge amounts of money while doing so. Amazingly, Americans spent more on meds last year, nearly $225 billion, than the federal government spent on education, transportation, agriculture and on the environment.

Let's first look at this issue in the context of depression, then we'll look at how it plays out with weight problems.

DEPRESSION

We need to beware of what is fast becoming the depression industry. Too many physicians have become a drug delivery system for pharmaceutical companies; 28 million Americans now take anti-depressant medications prescribed by their doctors. The pharmaceutical industry enjoys $6 billion (and rising) yearly in worldwide revenue from "anti-depressant" drugs. The idea that all depression represents a biological disease is a fiction that's falsely portrayed as fact, and millions of people who seek help from feelings of depression get fed the bogus story line and the expensive and potentially dangerous "medicines" along with it.

Drug companies market and promote the false idea that ALL depression is a brain problem or illness, and they often fund research to prove it. This story line is used to market and promote expensive and potentially very risky medication as the cure for feelings of depression. Unfortunately many physicians buy into this idea, no pun intended. The story line goes like this:

- Depression is an illness caused by chemical imbalances in the brain, an illness that requires medication to restore balance.
- My patient is depressed.
- My patient needs medication to restore their brain to chemical balance.

The truth is that no one knows what side effects the long-term use of anti-depressant medications will bring, and it is a well-known fact that the most serious ones are underreported by the drug companies and the FDA. Harvard psychiatrist Joseph Glenmullen raises questions about the unsettling concerns of risky side effects in his book <u>Prozac Backlash: Overcoming the Dangers of Prozac, Zoloft, Paxil, and Other Antidepressants</u>.

Moreover, reliable scientific research shows three things

that argue against medicating most depression:

1. The vast majority of people troubled by feelings of depression do not have a brain biochemistry problem.
2. Antidepressant medications are often no more effective than sugar pills in relieving symptoms.
3. Medication does nothing to address or change the real source of depression—chronic uncertainty based states of mind including fear, self-doubt, worry, anxiety and the stress hormones they produce.

The deepest causes of depression often result from our living at the Wrong Address. Our True Address, our Innermost Identity, is "de-pressed" or "pressed down" so low that it's not visible. I have seen again and again that when people suffering from non-biological depression learn and practice the Unshakable Certainty Process™, they discover that their depression is a coded message prompting them to stop living from their surface Self-Image. It's a call to Relocate to their True Address and live from there with gusto instead.

If a plant is denied sun, food and water, it wilts; if our inner identity is denied what it needs, if it's trapped—then it also sags, sinks and withers. People troubled by depression need to decode this message, not medicate it. Their inner identity needs to be seen, cared for and honored.

When they finally discover it, when they see more deeply who they truly are, their deeper identity will feel like a person lost at sea feels when, after much time and struggle, she is finally seen by the pilot of a rescue helicopter who failed to see her earlier, despite her calls and pleas.

The same reality generally applies to weight problems. There's truth to the saying that the real issue for overweight people isn't what they eat, it's what's eating them. Shaky uncertainty is what's eating them. And who they truly are, their deepest self, is starving and, like the cookie monster, it's calling and yelling "Feed Me!" Let's turn now to take a closer look at this call and what it can do to a person.

WEIGHT PROBLEMS

More than half of Americans are overweight, and 300,000 people die annually because of weight problems, second only to tobacco as a cause of preventable deaths. Obesity, or excess fat on the body, is considered as an epidemic in developing countries, countries where food is for many people the "drug" of choice because it's so available. Numerous high-risk medical conditions are now known to be linked to obesity, including heart disease, high blood pressure, stroke, some forms of cancer and type 2 diabetes. We should note here that these are the same medical conditions caused by the chronic release of stress hormones, hormones triggered by shaky uncertainty. The medical and pharmaceutical establishments consider obesity a long-term chronic disease, yet another illness for which they produce and market drugs to a weight-conscious public.

Although the drug companies have set up their marketing machinery around weight problems, there are fewer prescription drugs available than for depression. And the drugs that are available claim to suppress the appetite by affecting the brain in ways similar to antidepressants. Many of these drugs have clear side-effect dangers, and they can only be taken for brief periods of time and under close supervision.

With the lack of safe prescription drugs that work effectively, a tidal wave of diet pills, supplements and herbal weight loss products has hit the marketplace, although there's little valid experimental evidence that these products work or that they're safe. People spend many billions of dollars yearly on prescription and herbal diet pills, diet gurus, diet foods, diet books and diet programs—few if any of which really work, especially over the long haul. Yet the diet industry is immensely powerful and their marketing strategies work all too well. These strategies succeed in convincing people troubled by the way they look that they can continue to self-medicate shaky uncertainty with giant size plates of food and become thin and feel great at the same time.

Most of these weight-loss programs make billions in profits by misinforming the public; they sell the idea that people can eat as much as they want and stay slim and well. The Atkin's diet books have sold 15 million copies, and one more book with a trendy title called *The South Beach Diet* is yet another low carbohydrate plan, another plan that tells people they can eat their neighbor's house as long as it's not made of carbohydrates.

In the same way that good research on antidepressant medications has shown them to be ineffective or only marginally effective, research on the most popular fad diets has proven that their claim that you can eat plenty of calories—if they're the right kind of calories—is a claim made of hot air. The problem is that you cannot fool the calorie gods, as more than 30 years of medical literature on diets show. According to Walter Willett, Chairman of the Department of Nutrition at the Harvard School of Public Health, "The studies are clear. As far as body fat goes, it doesn't make any difference where your calories come from."

No fad diet or fad diet program addresses the real problem. These fad diets sell so well because they promise people that they can continue to medicate their shaky uncertainty with food, with their drug of choice. People in distress do not want to part with their drug, with the "medication" that gives them relief. They seek relief from feelings of fear, self-doubt, worry, anxiety, depression and insecurity, and from the Waking Dreams and toxic stress hormones that these feelings trigger.

They often feel tired, depleted, depressed and burnt out. Their energy is low and fades quickly, and they often don't look well or feel well. They regularly rely on food for relief from the stress and strain of uncertainty, including, for many people, high carbohydrate foods, foods that are particularly attractive when we're stressed out. Many people under high levels of stress eat too much or too often—or both.

And what they eat may cause weight problems because they're looking for a taste rush, not a healthy snack or meal, and so the inevitable weight gain that results can become yet another entrance into a Waking Dream of fear, uncertainty and self-doubt. Feeling and looking fat is a huge Briar Patch trigger. Moreover, stress hormones such as cortisol create a build-up of fatty deposits, especially around the midsection.

Once the pattern of "food as medication" becomes well established, it operates like an addiction, and it becomes a habitual method of dealing with the stressful Waking Dreams, dreams that are the result of living at one's Wrong Address. The only real and final solution for a person caught in this dilemma is to fully wake up to what's going on. And in the process of awakening, to connect to who they truly are and to the Unshakable Certainty that comes with it.

Once awake, then people can see food, not as medication, but as an opportunity to pleasure themselves consciously. As Frank Lloyd Wright, the legendary architect noted so well, "Dining is...a great artistic opportunity."

Let's now begin to close this chapter by examining a graphic representation that clearly shows the powerful relationship between Unshakable Certainty and health and well-being.

Unshakable Certainty	Shaky Uncertainty
Low Stress Levels Infrequent Release of Stress Hormones	High Stress Levels Chronic Release of Stress Hormones
Stress Hormones Flushed Out of Blood and Tissues Quickly and Thoroughly	Stress Hormones Seep into Blood and Tissues and Remain
Few Health Complaints and Problems Rarely Depressed and/or Overweight	Many Health Complaints and Problems Often Depressed and/or Overweight
Strong Immune System Colds Go Away Fast and Wounds Heal Quickly	Weakened Immune System Colds Linger and Wounds Heal Slowly
Reduced Incidence of Heart Disease and Cancer	Increased Incidence of Heart Disease and Cancer
High Energy, Upbeat, Optimistic, Happy, Anticipates Success	Low Energy, Depressed, Pessimistic, Unhappy, Anticipates Failure
Resorts to Calm and Relaxed State of Mind to Unwind	Resorts to Food and Mood Altering Substances to Unwind
Controlled Enjoyment of Food and Substances for Recreation and Pleasure	Out of Control Use of Food And Substances as Self-Medication to Elevate Mood and to Relieve Stress

A SUM OF THE BIG PICTURE

The quality of your health, your work and your relationships depend on one quintessential thing: Unshakable Certainty.

And Unshakable Certainty depends on a positive answer to one question: Are you awake? If you're awake, you can be vibrantly alive, you can be free to be who you deeply are, and you can live your life with gusto and wisdom according to your own vision—no one else's—and you can have profound joy and peace to boot.

The Unshakable Certainty Process™ is a surefire resource that will allow you to answer yes to the "Are you awake?" question. Aware Presence will bear great fruit in your life, there is no doubt. It will connect you to the experience of your life as part of the IMMENSITY that all life is.

Once connected, you'll know that who you are is in essence so breathtakingly real and valuable that you can let go of whatever is in the way of your happiness. To be happy is to live without fear, worry and self-doubt; it's to live and create from who you truly are.

The idea that you live at your Wrong Address is a way of pointing out how limited and hazardous your conditioning can be to your life. Your True Address is awake. It is unshakably certain awareness, Aware Presence. It lies beyond conditioned influences of any kind. But the goal is not to divorce yourself from who you know yourself to be and take up complete residence in some delicate and insubstantial state of mind called awareness.

You're not out to destroy your Wrong Address, rather you're out to change it in light of awareness, in light of Unshakable Certainty. You want a revolution in the way you live, nothing less, but it's not a destructive revolution—it's a creative one. Your Wrong Address and Aware Presence are not enemies or opponents—in truth they are part of the same life. Your Surface Identity is only your Wrong Address if it operates without awareness, if it lives in Waking Dreams. Not only can your Surface Identity grow in light of awareness, but it can become its voice.

When Aware Presence and Unshakable Certainty become

your loyal companions, your life will be enriched beyond measure, because they will be such good companions that they will
allow you to always be aware of the gold standard quality of life
question: In view of infinity does this state of mind I am in
really matter?

CHAPTER 10
Elvis Lives On

"Our Destiny is always present, although never completely visible until we remember who we truly are.
...Remembrance is a form of grace. It is the grace that
arises from awareness...."

—Bruce Nelson

AN ELVIS STORY

Elvis Presley was widely considered by millions to be the undisputed King of Rock and Roll. He was indeed an amazing performer, particularly in his prime. Although he died more than 25 years ago, Elvis lives on in the hearts of his fans, some of whom swear that he is still alive. These fans regularly report Elvis sightings. They see him in parking lots, at movies and more than a few have seen the King while scuba diving in 50 feet of very fishy water.

Fred Linton, the owner of a small music store outside of Portland, Oregon is a passionate music lover. He is a big Elvis fan who took things a step further. Not only had he seen Elvis many times, but now he was convinced of something even more astounding. <u>Fred believes he IS Elvis.</u> Here's his story.

Fred wakes up one morning convinced that he is Elvis Presley. After jumping out of bed and singing, "You Ain't Nothin' but a Hound Dog," he turns to his wife and demands that she treat him with the respect due the King of Rock and Roll. At breakfast Fred makes the same demand of his two children, and later at work that day, of his business partner and employees.

Initially, they all get a kick out of Fred's bizarre behavior, but by week's end, they've had enough.

They conclude that the best way to expose Fred's folly is to hire a lie detector expert. They reason that once a lie detector proves that Fred is not Elvis, this foolishness will end.

Somehow, Fred gets wind of their scheme.

Upset and disappointed, he decides to spoil their plan by denying that he is Elvis.

On the appointed day, everyone arrives at lie detector expert's office, on the 27th floor of the LVR Windows Building. All are eager for the test to begin.

The expert begins with obligatory questions. She asks Fred: How old are you? What town do you live in? What's your shoe size? And so on.

Then the lie detector expert asks the key question: "Are you Elvis Presley?"

To everyone's surprise, Fred answers, "No." But even more flabbergasting are the results.

So deep is Fred's conviction that he is Elvis Presley that <u>the lie detector reads that Fred is lying when he says that he isn't</u>.

The group is shocked with disbelief, but Fred is elated, for no one can dispute the truth any longer. Elvis Lives!

On the way down, Fred's elevator gets stuck between floors.

Fred thinks he might as well make the best of the situation so he quivers his upper lip and says to the other passengers: "Hi, I'm Elvis Presley and I'd be happy to sing a few songs for you all while we're waiting to get out of here."

"Whaat? Huh? C'mon, Elvis is dead"—The voices reply.

Fred responds, "No really, I am Elvis, the test proved it." He then belts out a chorus of Jail House Rock.

Then a gentle female voice from the corner whispers:

"Hello Fred, I am Steadfast Knowledge. Wake up!"

"What do you mean wake up, my eyes are open and I'm wide awake"

"You're in a Waking Dream," Steadfast Knowledge replies. "That's why you believe that you are something that you are not. I know what you're feeling feels real—but it isn't."

A male voice disagrees. "I dunno, he sounds like Elvis to me."

"Thank you for your support," says Fred. "When we get out of here, I'll give you an autographed photo. What's your name?"

"Safeguard," the man replies.

"Now wait a minute," Steadfast Knowledge objects. "Safeguard wants you to feel safe, but he doesn't understand that it's not in your best interests to be stuck in a dream."

"But I am committed to his best interests," Safeguard replies defensively.

"Safeguard, you know very well that Fred is not Elvis Presley; why do you allow him to think he is?"

"Because it makes him feel better, it makes him feel safe, and if he feels safe then he's OK. And that's all I want is for him to feel safe and OK."

Steadfast Knowledge fires back, "If you want him to be okay, then you have to join me and help him to wake up. He's not safe in this dream. Together we need to help him to answer an important question."

Tensely, Fred bursts in, "And just what question is that?"

"Why are you afraid to be who you are?" Steadfast Knowledge asks tenderly.

Fred suddenly feels a rush of anxiety he can't understand. It is as if he is stark naked in the middle of a brightly lit room. But he trusts this woman.

"I don't know. But it sure feels good to be Elvis; it doesn't feel good to be me."

"But you're not safe being Elvis; it wasn't even safe for Elvis to be Elvis. It's never safe to be someone you're not."

"Well then who am I?"

"That's the big question, Fred. I want you and Safeguard to really listen now, because I want you to know who you are, and I want Safeguard to know exactly who to protect. OK?

"Sure, OK."

"When your wife comes home and calls out, "Where are you Fred?" depending on what room you're in, you might answer, 'in the kitchen or in the living room or in the bathroom' right?"

"Yup."

"Well your mind is your inner home. And your mind has different rooms in it. Elvis is one room and the 'me' that you don't like being is another room in your mind. Understand?"

"Yes, very clearly."

"Good. So now let me ask you: Where are you Fred?"

"I am in the elevator with you and Safeguard."

"No Fred, where are you in your mind? Are you in the Elvis room or in the 'me room' or in some other room?"

"Well if you put it that way, I'm just LOOKING at both of these rooms, but I'm not IN either of them."

"That's good Fred. You just made my task a lot easier. Listen— the place in you that 'sees' these rooms without being in them is called awareness, and that's who you really are."

"Awareness?"

"That's right Fred, awareness, just being and seeing what's happening Now.

Some people call it being in the present, being in the Now or being in the moment. The bottom line is when you are simply being aware, you are being your true self and that's the safest place you can be."

"But how do I stay aware?" Fred asks.

"Well for one thing, always know that you are NEVER the room you're in, though it will often seem that way. Next, know that you are ALWAYS the awareness that 'sees' what room you're in."

"That's a little tricky, but I think I get it," announces Safeguard.

"Me too, but what do I do when I'm stuck in one of those rooms?"

"Just remember—to ask yourself—'Where Am I Now?' Always strive to know where you are. That question always triggers a sliver of awareness. It's a call to yourself to wake up. Next use the connection between the mind and body to breathe free. Take a deep breath and on the out breath —let go completely."

"Then what?"

"Then tune yourself to the relaxed awareness at the end of the breath. This kind of out breath is a slide that you go down to enter into the Now. In the space between the out breath and the next in breath, you'll find calm, clear awareness. Let the sliver of awareness flow into that larger pool of awareness so that it can become more stable."

"Sounds tough."

"Not at all Fred; the more you do it, the easier it gets—you just have to practice. With practice, awareness becomes like a good friend who gives you his address so you can find him when you need to."

"Hey wait just a minute, what about me?" An angry voice butts in.

"Who the heck are you?" asks Fred.

"I'm Briar Patch, and all this talk about breaking free and relocating is making me pretty angry. Bad enough Safeguard stuck me in a dark hole years ago, now you're just gonna leave me?"

Safeguard adds, "I cannot tell a lie, I did it."

"But why?" Fred asks.

"So you'd feel safe and stay OK. You were in big trouble. So I gathered some of your pain and heartache and I wrapped it up and buried it in a hole."

"Fred, you need to spend some time with Briar Patch and get to know him," adds Steadfast Knowledge.

"But he makes me uncomfortable."

"Is that why you always leave me?" Briar Patch asks Fred in anger.

"Yes, because if I don't avoid or leave you—I become you."

"But Fred I need you. I feel like no one really loves me and that I am funny-looking and slow and so very alone."

"Yes, yes I know, but when I fall into you, I feel that way too and it leaves me pretty shaky and uncertain."

"Yes, and so now you're gonna wake up, relocate and just abandon me."

In her soft and soothing voice, Steadfast Knowledge asks Fred and Briar Patch, "Can I say something boys?"

"Sure," they reply.

"Fred's not going to abandon you, Briar Patch. He's learning how to find himself, and how to stay himself so he can be with you instead of becoming you."

She turns to Fred and goes on. "Fred you have two choices. You can keep falling into Briar Patch for the rest of your life or you can get to know him. He needs your help."

"How come I get so anxious when I am around him?"

"Because he's what you don't want to know about yourself."

Safeguard jumps in at this point. "I just keep worrying that if he comes out of his hole and into the light of day, then you'll fall apart. So I keep the anxiety high so you'll stay away."

Steadfast Knowledge replies, "Yes that's true. But now I want you to know something very important: The danger that was _then_ *is not the danger that is <u>now</u>."*

"But it feels that way. When Fred's mom was drinking she yelled at him and told him he was stupid and ugly."

"No wonder why I want to be Elvis. Everyone loves and respects Elvis."

"It gets worse Fred," Safeguard adds. "She belittled you in front of your friends and it hurt you so much you used to apologize for looking funny. If I didn't give you some Novocain for your pain, you were in big, big trouble."

"You were a great protector Safeguard, but now I want you and Fred to learn a whole other level of being safe. It's based on awareness, not on running away or hiding. Understand?"

"Yes," Safeguard replies knowingly.

Steadfast Knowledge continues. "Briar Patch needs help. He's not funny-looking or slow or unworthy of love and respect—but he thinks he is. When Fred falls into him—he falls into a Waking Dream based on these feelings."

Fred breaks in. "Yes, that's exactly right. That's where I need to wake up and relocate to awareness."

"Yes, but what about ME?" yells Briar Patch.

"Don't worry. He's coming back for you, like I told you."

"He'd better. I keep sending him messages but he ignores them. I make him anxious shaky and depressed. That's the only way I can call to him, but he ignores me. I NEED help."

Fred then says, "OK I get it, Steadfast Knowledge, tell me when do I go back for Briar Patch?"

"Only after you connect with awareness, otherwise you'll become him. When you're aware, you go back and talk with him"

"Talk with him?"

"Yes, treat Briar Patch like an invisible guest—with caring and respect. Take him out for a talk, for a 'meaningful conversation.'"

"What shall I talk to Briar Patch about?"

"Let him tell you his story. Care for him. Then slowly you can help free him from the false ideas that hurt him so much."

Safeguard steps in excitedly. "I see now what this is all about. I don't need to help Fred hide from his Briar Patches any longer."

"Exactly, now your job of protecting him has been upgraded to one mission: Help him stay awake. Your work is to help him stay connected to who he truly is—awareness."

"This is awesome; where'd you learn all this?"

"Awareness taught me."

"Excuse us but we're dying to say hello; can we jump in here?"

"Who are you?" Fred blurts out astonished that so many characters can fit in one elevator.

"We are the Free Position and Aware Presence, two sides of the same coin. We follow Steadfast Knowledge wherever she goes."

Fred asks, "You feel like old friends but at the same time, I don't know you. Who are you?"

"I am awareness with no agenda. I have no hopes or fears. I allow everything to just be what it is. Sure you know me; I am your deepest nature," replies the Free Position.

"How can that possibly be?" Fred asks.

Steadfast Knowledge breaks in and says to Fred, "Free Position is like a mirror that remains unaffected by anything that comes before it."

"That is correct, and so as long as you are connected to me, you are awake and completely free."

Fred, nearly beside himself in excitement turns to Steadfast Knowledge and asks, "All of this is now as clear as a bell, so why do I get lost in dreams so much?"

"You get lost in dreams because your attention follows what the mirror reflects, not what the mirror is."

Aware Presence bursts in and in a hauntingly clear voice says to Fred, *"And if you are aware and present, then you remain awake and connected to what the mirror is. There is no Unshakable Certainty beyond that—it is the very last word."*

Suddenly the elevator starts up and heads down, though the lights remain out. Steadfast Knowledge then says in a hurried but tender voice, "Fred we must stop. But keep one last thing in mind. Fear, self-doubt, hesitation, insecurity, anxiety, depression are all reflections."

"Yes, yes, I see that now."

"Don't follow them, stay awake, but don't abandon them either—ever—go back for them always."

The lights go on and everyone heads again toward the ground floor. Fred looks around in total shock because he realizes that he is alone in the elevator. He staggers out and he feels very unsettled. Until he hears a familiar voice.

Steadfast Knowledge whispers into his inner ear: "Forget Elvis, Fred—find and sing your own song—you old hound dog you."

A FINAL NOTE

As you can see, the stakes are high. We either live our life in an ongoing series of Waking Dreams driven by shaky uncertainty, or we find Unshakable Certainty and live our life as an adventure of love, courage, well-being, wisdom and meaningful accomplishment.

Most of us can see and feel this truth when our eyes are wide open, when special moments in life somehow connect us to our Innermost Identity and our fears, self-doubts and worries just seem to evaporate in the warmth and power of who we truly are.

While in this state of "knowing," you can promise yourself to live your life as an adventure, but you may not really know how to seize this window of opportunity.

And so the problem is that because your Wrong Address is so wired in as the default position of who you are—you forget. Your knowledge is not yet steadfast; it depends on your being in a special state of mind. When you're not in that state of mind, you can lose your awareness of who you deeply are and what the View is from there. Not only do you forget, but worse still— you forget that you've forgotten—and then all is lost. The fire of awareness and knowledge goes out.

The Unshakable Certainty Process™ keeps the fire going. It will keep your awareness and knowledge heated up enough so that they are no longer dependent on states of mind that you can't access at will, on states of mind that inevitably fade and grow cold. If you learn and practice the Process, then when you want to wake up and connect to Unshakable Certainty, you can throw a log onto hot burning coals instead of having to start a fire cold from scratch.

Don't let finishing this book put your fire out. There's no doubt that you can find Unshakable Certainty, but only if you want to. Practice the Process within the bounds of what you understand, keep the big picture in mind and feel it with your heart.

If you'd like to experience Unshakable Certainty as a way of life, I recommend that you master the 5-Step dance of the Process so that it becomes fluid and second nature to you. If you do, there's no doubt that it will change your life. Most of the many people who've mastered the Process and who enjoy its greatest fruits are people who learn it through expert training, support and guidance.

A program of training, support and guidance will enable you to expertly understand what the Process is and how to use it. Then you can use it in your daily life with skill, confidence—and powerful results. I have personally trained all program staff members so that they are fully prepared to help you to master using the Process in your unique life circumstances.

Contact me for information on getting the expert training, support and supervision you need to master the Process to find and live from Unshakable Certainty.

Call me at: 800 434-9025

Or you can contact me through my Uncommon Knowledge Radio site: www.WUKR.com

APPENDIX 1

GLOSSARY

Aware Presence
Briar Patch
Free Position
Hosting
Innermost Identity
Location
LVR
Mapping
Safeguard
Self-Image
Surface Identity
Steadfast Knowledge
True Psychological Address
Waking Dream

AWARE PRESENCE- the clear, calm, awakened state of mind that is the foundation of Unshakable Certainty. It is pure, impartial, and simultaneous here and now awareness; it has no agenda or attachment to outcomes of any kind. Aware Presence is our deepest nature. We need to first find it, and then become 100% sure about what it is, and then we need to cultivate and stabilize it. The UC Process™ allows us to do exactly that so we can live and create from Unshakable Certainty.

BRIAR PATCH- is an unseen and unknown patch of emotional territory within your mind, territory you can fall into and get stuck in. You get stuck in a Briar Patch Location easily because it's filled with the thorny hurts, wounds and feelings from your past. A Briar Patch lies dormant outside your awareness until it's triggered. Then it comes to life and, without realizing what's happening, you can fall into it and become possessed by its View and Reality.

FREE POSITION- is the flip side of Aware Presence. It's the Unshakable Certainty Location—wide open and without fixed Views of any kind. Its Reality is always—clear, calm, open, free and aware. When you are in the Free Position, you are aware and present—you're awake—here and now. Like a pond that reflects the images of birds that fly over it without becoming affected or changed by them, when you are in the Free Position, you can host thoughts and feelings without being defined by them.

HOSTING-is the ability to be aware of a state of mind from the Free Position, from an aware, impartial Location other than that state of mind. When you can host a troublesome state of mind such as fear and self doubt, you can deliteralize and relativize it so that it presents itself as one LVR among others—rather than as the literal and absolute truth.

INNERMOST IDENTITY- is your True Address—it's your real face. It's who you are in your deepest being, beyond family or cultural conditioning. It's where you find Unshakable Certainty based on the ability to simply be who you are.

LOCATION-is where you are psychologically in any given moment. Your state of mind is your Location—it's "where you are now." If you are depressed, for example, your depressed state of mind is a Location. Every Location carries with it a View and every View defines an experience of Reality.

LVR- Location, View and Reality. Your Location determines your View. Your View defines your Reality. Your Reality is your experience of what is real

MAPPING- is the activity of discovering, exploring and becoming familiar with the forces at play within your psychology, especially your Self-Image and your Briar Patch LVR's. Mapping is part of the inner work you do to gather the self-knowledge you need to create the necessary foundation for Unshakable Certainty. What remains unmapped in you can ambush you around any corner and toss you into shaky uncertainty.

SAFEGUARD- is the personification of the security and protection forces within your personality. He cuts you off from difficult experiences and threats, particularly during childhood, so you can maintain your equilibrium. The problem is that what he cuts you off from becomes a Briar Patch that remains stuck in past time. Because of Safeguard's preoccupations, you often see the present in terms of the past. Steadfast Knowledge (see below) re-educates Safeguard and brings him and you into present time.

SELF-IMAGE- is an image of who you are based on ideas downloaded from your family about your physical and psychological characteristics, about your intelligence and abilities and about your value and worthiness as a human being. Your Self-Image develops in accord with how significant others "saw" you during your formative years. Although your Self-Image is based on others' views of you, you still come to think of it as who you really are, as your "I" or "me". It becomes your Surface Identity and your Wrong Psychological Address. Your Self-Image is so powerful that whether or not it's accurate—you'll think, feel and act in accord with it.

STEADFAST KNOWLEDGE- the center of gravity based on the experiential self-knowledge you develop using the UC Process™. Steadfast Knowledge is the Mother of Unshakable Certainty. She turns the lights on so you can see what is and, in time, she leaves them on.

SURFACE IDENTITY- your Wrong Psychological Address. Your conditioned Self-Image based identity. See above.

TRUE PSYCHOLOGICAL ADDRESS- your deeper and more essential identity. See Innermost Identity.

WAKING DREAMS- are what happens when you are not aware of your Location and you're caught up and identified with that Location's View and Reality. Like a sleeping dream, a Waking Dream presents itself as literally true and real (e.g. a crocodile chasing you in a sleeping dream feels real—until you wake up). When you become aware of your Waking Dream Location, then you realize it determines your View and your View defines your Reality or what you think is real. You become aware that your experience is always relative to where you are within yourself.

APPENDIX 2

A QUICK GRAPHIC SUMMARY
OF ALL AND EVERYTHING

The tables below offers a quick but comprehensive reference for everything we've examined relating to Unshakable Certainty and about the difference between a life lived with it and one lived without it. The tables can work nicely for you as a reminder of how the dots are connected and of exactly what the stakes are.

Location, View and Reality	
SHAKY UNCERTAINTY	UNSHAKABLE CERTAINTY
Wrong Address	True Address
Surface Identity	Innermost Identity
Conditioned Self-Image=Default	View Free Position=Default View
Fixed and Inflexible Views	Open and Flexible Views
Emotional Confusion	Steadfast Knowledge
Unmapped Briar Patches	Mapped Briar Patches
Uneducated Safeguard	Educated Safeguard
Mustard Forgotten	Mustard Remembered
Possessed by Views	Hosts Views
Waking Dreams	Aware Presence

Work	
SHAKY UNCERTAINTY	UNSHAKABLE CERTAINTY
Work Based on Should or Must	Work Based on Want and Love
Work Rooted in Conditioning	Work Based on Unique Purpose
Work as Obligation	Work as Adventure
Work is Boring	Work is Fulfilling
Work is Exhausting	Work is Energizing
Challenges=Big Problems	Challenges=Nice Opportunities
Work has Little or No Meaning	Work has Significant Meaning
Little Focus	Laser-Like Focus
Work as Drudgery	Work as Play

Relationships

SHAKY UNCERTAINTY	UNSHAKABLE CERTAINTY
Conscious Love Absent	Conscious Love Central
Focus on Self	Focus on Other
Love and Friendship Blocked	Love and Friendship Flowing
Ego Based Relationship	Heart Based Relationship
Closed Briar Patch Ceasefires	Open Meaningful Conversation
I—He or She is Bad and Wrong	No One is Bad and Wrong
Win/Lose Conflict	Win/Win Conflict
Challenges=Bad Problems	Challenges=Nice Opportunities
Relationship a Parking Spot	Relationship an Adventure
Alienated Family Life	Meaningful Family Life

Health and Well-Being

SHAKY UNCERTAINTY	UNSHAKABLE CERTAINTY
High Stress Views	Low Stress Views
Stress Hormones Remain	Stress Hormones Flush Out
Many Health Complaints	Few Health Complaints
Infirmity and Early Death	Well-Being and Longevity
Often Depressed	Rarely Depressed
Often Overweight	Rarely Overweight
Compromised Immune System	Strong Immune System
More Heart Problems	Fewer Heart Problems
Low Energy and Downbeat	High Energy and Upbeat
Pessimistic and Unhappy	Optimistic and Happy
Anticipates Failure	Anticipates Success
Eating as Self-Medication	Eating as Healthy Pleasure